Free Riding
in
Avalanche Terrain
A Snowboarder's Handbook

Bruce Jamieson

and

Jennie McDonald

Published by

CANADIAN
AVALANCHE
ASSOCIATION

P.O. Box 2759, Revelstoke, BC V0E 2S0 Canada

Phone 1-250-837-2435, Fax 1-250-837-4624

e-mail: canav@avalanche.ca

http://www.avalanche.ca/

ISBN 0-9685856-0-4

Printed in Canada

©1999 J. Bruce Jamieson

Calgary, Alberta, Canada

Design by Snowline Technical Services

Layout by Torsten Geldsetzer

Front cover photo by Dan Hudson. Rider Karleen Jeffery.

Back cover photos (top and bottom) by Dan Hudson. Rider Matt Goodwill.

Back cover background of Kokanee Mountain courtesy of Columbia Brewery

Illustrations and photos by Bruce Jamieson, except as indicated

Edited by Julie Lockhart, Wind Word Consulting

Printed in Canada by Kromar Printing Ltd.

Canadian Cataloguing in Publication Data

Jamieson, James Bruce.
  Free riding in avalanche terrain

  Includes bibliographical references.
  ISBN 0-9685856-0-4

  1. Snowboarding--Safety measures. 2. Avalanches--Safety measures. I. McDonald, Jennie, 1979- II. Canadian Avalanche Association. III. Title
QC929.A8J35 1999   796.9   C99-911007-1

Acknowledgements

This book was a team effort. Richard Rotteveel and Evan Manners from the Canadian Avalanche Centre started the process and provided ongoing support. Columbia Brewery, Burton Snowboards and Survival on Snow provided financial support when this book was only a concept. Robert Conn from the Smartrisk Foundation and Walter Bruns from Canadian Mountain Holidays stimulated our thinking about risk and training. Dan Hudson, Jim Bay, Neil Brown, John Buffery, James Blench, Rob Orvig and Selkirk Mountain Experience provided great photos. Robin Siggers and Gordon Ohm from Fernie Alpine Resort as well as Parker McDonald, Nick Irving and Jill Hughes helped with photo sessions. Dan Hudson wrote the first person account for the Mt. Baker avalanche and rescue. John Buffery, Neil Brown, Dan Hudson, Phil Hein, Craig Kelly and Randy Stevens made very helpful comments on a draft of this book. Gwyn Howat from Mount Baker Ski Area gave constructive comments on Chapter 2. Torsten Geldsetzer did the final layout and coordinated the printing.

We are very grateful for all the help we received during this project.

Bruce Jamieson and Jennie McDonald

Table of Contents

Preface

This is the third book in the Canadian Avalanche Association's series on reducing the avalanche risk for backcountry recreationists. It is compatible with the Canadian Avalanche Association's course outlines and instructional materials for Recreational Avalanche Courses.

We have used superscripts like this[1] to mark facts and ideas from other sources. In some cases these references may help readers dig deeper into the subject, but we also want to recognize the contributions of others to avalanche training.

In a few years, this book will be revised. We look forward to comments from readers and avalanche instructors.

Jennie McDonald had her start in what many riders dream of—cruising the powderfields of the Rockies. With day to day access by sled, snowcat and snowshoe under the guidance of seasoned mountain guides, she developed a healthy fear of the snow. After learning to ski, she started riding in 1992 (age 13) and has been a Burton rider since 1996. Her first inspiration for snow science was the CAA Level 1 course. She now looks to the future to keep her mountain skills sharp by blending experience from traditional CASI snowboard instructing with snow science in her frequent backcountry excursions.

Bruce Jamieson has been working with avalanches for the last 22 years: avalanche control, forecasting, teaching, writing, researching and consulting. A past president of the Canadian Avalanche Association, he has written or co-written three previous books on avalanches. His current research on avalanche prediction involves field studies in the Columbia Mountains. A long time backcountry skier, he now prefers snowboarding when the snow is soft and the fall line is sustained.

Chapter 1
Introduction

Free riding in the mountains away from ski areas involves risk, including avalanche risk. Reduce the risk to a level you are comfortable with—and you can't beat riding in the backcountry.

This book is about techniques for reducing avalanche risk, and it's about choice. Snowboarders and others who enjoy the mountains are constantly choosing routes and lines—each with a level of risk at any time. A particular gully might be high risk today and lower risk tomorrow. And the open slope beside the gully *might* be low risk today. In the backcountry, you can decide where and when to go. Backcountry riding offers untracked lines, soft snow and choice.

Much of the great free riding in the backcountry is in avalanche terrain. We can ignore the avalanche conditions and accept the high risk. Or we can assess the snow conditions and pick routes that suit the current conditions   low risk routes. Some days we will have to avoid some great slopes. Under better conditions, we'll ride those same slopes. Occasionally, we may have to pass on the backcountry and ride in a ski area.

This book includes techniques to reduce our exposure to avalanches when we are in the backcountry— going up and riding down. We also need to carry rescue gear and know how to use it.

These techniques will help us ride in the backcountry, year after year. However, avalanche knowledge and decision-making skills take time to develop and refine. So, choose your routes with caution while developing your skills and knowledge.

This book is not a substitute for an avalanche course. While avalanche training is strongly recommended, keep in mind that avalanche books and courses cover only the basics of recognizing unstable snow and assessing avalanche danger. Afterwards, much remains to be learned from experienced riders, avalanche professionals, the snowpack and the mountains.

Dan Hudson photo.
Rider Jennie McDonald.

Chapter 2
Twenty Seconds

First Person Account of an Avalanche and Rescue

Story and photos by Dan Hudson

I stood and watched in awe as a massive wall of snow traveling at more than two hundred kilometers per hour swept through a gully just outside the Mt. Baker Ski Area boundary. No matter how many times I had read stories, seen photos, or watched videos of avalanches, there was nothing that could have prepared me for the destructive power of the real thing. There was also nothing that could have prepared me for the recurring nightmares I have experienced ever since I helped remove the cold stiff body of a young man from deep within the avalanche debris.

Avalanches are like having a psycho go on a killing spree in your neighborhood. It is a shocking occurrence to most people but predictable to those who had been paying attention to the telltale signs. Such was the case with the avalanche at Mt. Baker.

This incident could have just as easily been at almost any mountain resort in North America. It was not a freak accident. It was a classic slab avalanche on a steep, convex slope and it released on a predicted weak layer.

Snowfall was well above average in the Mt. Baker area at the time of the incident.

The area that avalanched has a long history of sliding. As a matter of fact, another snowboarder was still buried in Rumble Gully from a slide three weeks earlier.

Recognizing when it is safe to go into the backcountry is the key to survival. Sure, you could be an awesome snowboarder and have no trouble ripping the terrain out of bounds, but that doesn't necessarily mean that you understand snowpack dynamics.

Avalanches really don't care how great a snowboarder you are.

We were able to remove our packs at this windlip because there was no avalanche danger in this area. Moments after Darren Dickinson landed this air we heard a big crack and turned to see the avalanche rip out of the nearby slope.

That busy Sunday was the first nice day the Mt. Baker area had seen in months. Early in the morning, myself (a photographer) and three pro snowboarders joined a seemingly endless stream of people climbing out of bounds, straight up from Chair 8. The hill was crowded and the locals were escaping to the backcountry in force. This just goes to disprove two popular myths: (1) that good weather has anything to do with snow stability. (2) That all locals always know what they are doing.

> I never consider tracks, either up, or down, as signs of intelligent life.

From the top of the ridge you can go left along Shuksan Arm or to the right, toward Hemispheres. We were heading out the "Arm" to a mellow T ridge to take some air shots at a windlip. Not exactly the kind of gnarly steep terrain that makes great photos, but I knew it would be safe there. If there is one thing that I have learned over the years, it is that you can't always do what you really want to do in the backcountry. It doesn't necessarily mean that you have to be totally shut down when the avalanche conditions are bad. If you are smart about your terrain choice and make sure there is no danger from above, you could build a booter and still have a super fun day. That is exactly what we were intending to do.

I had checked the Internet for the avalanche conditions before I went to Baker and further checked with Patrol before I headed out into the backcountry. The consensus was grim. There had been rain in December followed by cold weather in January, then it had snowed steadily ever since. About 25 cm (10") a day for a month. The previous three weeks had reaped 6 meters (20') of storm snow. The entire snowpack was sitting on a crust layer with facetted snow. In other words, the avalanche danger was high and the instability was deep. Strangely, very few locals seemed aware of this fact.

Mt. Baker, like most resorts, has a backcountry avalanche posting at the lodge. Whether or not I think I may be heading out of bounds, I make it a standard practice to read the avalanche bulletin as soon as I arrive at any resort.

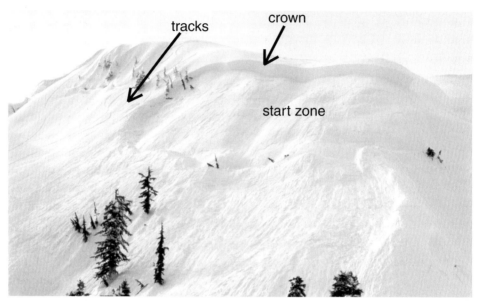

tracks

crown

start zone

Start zone and crown of the avalanche above Rumble Gully. Notice the tracks to the left of the start zone. The crown is more than 3 m (10') high.

As we hiked along the "Arm" a cloud band rolled in and we were whited out. It was the kind of day that the clouds would come and go so we pushed on.

We came across three snowboarders getting ready to drop in at the first high point of the ridge. They all had packs and avalanche gear but when I approached them to discuss the conditions they didn't really know what was going on. As they stood on top of a big cornice, they politely explained to me that they were locals and that they knew what they were doing. Furthermore, they had ridden that line many times before.

I agreed with them that the line was undoubtedly the best line up there. "Of course," I said, "that would be my first choice for a line as well, but for me, it is not worth the risk. Not today. Not with these conditions." I said goodbye, and we continued on.

It was slow going, busting trail along the ridge and when I looked back, I noticed that the three snowboarders had removed their boards and were following us out toward some safer terrain. They should be commended, not only forfeiting the line they had hiked for, but also for not being too proud or stubborn to change their plans when the conditions dictated it. It would have been a tough call to make, but I'm sure they are not regretting it now since their original line turned out to be on the very slope that avalanched two hours later.

It was 12:30 when I heard a big crack behind me. I had just used up the last frame in my camera when I turned around and saw the entire convex face of the steep slope between us and the ski resort disintegrate. The ground was shaking like an earthquake and the sound of full-size trees snapping in half could be heard above the roar of

start zone

Looking up the deposit at Rumble Gully after the avalanche. Note the start zone almost a km (half mile) away. The deposit is more than 15 m (50') deep!

the massive wave of snow. The avalanche quickly picked up speed and dumped into Rumble Gully as huge billows of snow accelerated down the drainage. Trees, 15 m (50') on either side of the actual rubble path, were bent and broken by the avalanche and its windblast. The crown was more than 3 m (10') deep and spanned about 80 m (250') across. Top to bottom, the avalanche ran for about a kilometer (0.6 mile). I didn't have time to get a single photo. My camera takes 15 seconds to rewind and after 20 seconds there was nothing but some snow dust left to settle.

Even though it is out of bounds, Rumble Gully is easily accessed from Chair 8 but you have to either pass under a ski area boundary rope-line or pass by a large backcountry sign which tells you of the dangers of leaving the ski area. Access to the backcountry area requires very little hiking. This area is also extremely popular because there are no trees—a consequence of previous avalanches. It made me feel sick to think of the number of people that could have been down there on that busy Sunday. Whatever I felt, it was nothing compared to what Mike Adams[*] must have felt.

"It just buried him alive," Adams said about his son Josh.

Mike had been celebrating his 44th birthday by snowboarding with his 19 year old son. The father was 50 m (150') behind his son when: "The whole hill swallowed my boy. I knew Josh was under there. I knew it was all over. There was nothing that I could do."

---

[*] The names in this account have been changed to protect the privacy of the family.

The probe line of 14 people covers only a small portion of the width of the deposit.

Neither of the Adams had transceivers, probes, shovels or avalanche safety training. Rumble Gully is such a popular run that they probably barely recognized that, by ducking under the boundary rope and passing by the backcountry warning sign, they were entering the backcountry.

Mike later mentioned that, "Josh had talked about 'pointing it' and riding out of an avalanche if the situation ever arose."

"That is exactly what he tried to do as I watched him," Mike related, "but he was like an ant trying to outrun a freight train. It just mowed him down. He didn't stand a chance."

Since I have some basic avalanche rescue training, I hurried to join in on any search effort that may have been mounted. It was too dangerous for me to ride across slope to the slide so I made my way down along the top of ridges and around the avalanche debris to the bottom of Chair 8.

As I was riding up the lift I was able to survey the full scope of the devastation. The debris was 15 m (50') deep in spots with chucks of snow the size of cars. There were bits and pieces of trees sticking out everywhere.

The chair seemed to take forever. Once I finally got to the top, I descended into the gully to join a probe line that the Mt. Baker Ski Patrol had organized. There were two confirmed victims (a snowboarder and a skier) and possibly more. A transceiver search had already been conducted by the time I arrived. No results.

I was probing at the end of a crew of volunteers. We were lined up like soldiers being instructed to do a fine probe with a ski patroller holding a rope at either end. A patroller named John was at my end yelling orders down the line like a drill sergeant, "Probes up!" Then they would move the rope forward a foot and the line would advance. "Probes down! Probes left! Probes right!"

Mike Adams had given the last known location of his son, so we were probing down the fall line from there. Progress was slow and tedious in the massive field of debris.

With almost every probe I made, I would hit hard chunks of snow and ice or pieces of broken trees. I wasn't sure if it would even be possible to identify a person down there. The hope of finding a survivor was dwindling as time passed so John made the call to speed things up by changing to a coarse probe.

Everyone was then instructed to only probe straight down, every two feet. It made it more likely to miss a buried person but more ground would be covered.

Shortly after that my heart jumped when I discovered the unmistakable feel of a person buried deep in the snow. I had pushed my probe in about as far as it would go when I hit the victim.

I was tongue-tied and the only thing I could get out of my mouth was, "Got one!" as if I just caught a fish.

I left my probe in the snow and grabbed another probe from the guy beside me to confirm the strike. There was no doubt about it. Someone from Ski Patrol ran over and confirmed it as well.

We busted out the shovels and started to dig like mad. There were about ten diggers working in shifts like a hockey team. The hole was getting deeper and wider. Eventually we had three teams going with snow being moved from one level to the next.

You have to make a big cone shaped hole to get ten feet down. I had re-moved my jacket and the sweat from my forehead was stinging my eyes as it ran down my face. I had used up all

Shoveling for the victim, while probing continues in the background.

my water earlier in the backcountry and was getting really thirsty. I was surprised at how thoroughly exhausting the digging was. Each time I got to the point that I could barely lift the shovel I would call for a replacement and someone else would jump in the hole. After a few minutes I would be right back in there. Everyone was pouring his or her heart into it. I hate to think how long it would take to dig a hole like that if it was just me and a couple of buddies out in the backcountry by ourselves.

Since the hole was so large, we had to remove the probe. At one point, it seemed that we were deeper than the length of the probe. I was beginning to have doubts that I had actually even found a person when we finally reached the victim's head. We quickly cleared the snow away.

The blank stare and gray colored skin of that face still haunts me. He looked like an old man. The ski patrollers went through the routine of resuscitation but I think it was obvious to everyone that our efforts had been in vain.

Mike Adams was called over to identify the body. "Oh God," he wailed, "that's my boy." "He is in God's hands now." He just kept repeating those three sentiments over and over as we continued to dig.

Josh Adams' body was pretzeled, but more or less vertical in the snow. We still had to dig almost 1.5 m (5') further down which took another 20 minutes. It was obvious that his snowboard had acted like an anchor. His board also made it hard to get him out. We were eventually able to cut through the straps and pull Josh's body out of the hole.

Meanwhile, the search for the young skier was called off 500 m (500 yards) down the gully due to increasing avalanche danger in the area. His sunglasses and hat were found right on the surface and one of his skis was located up in a tree, 10 m (30') from the edge of the slide path.

The skier's best friend had witnessed the entombment of his buddy and wasn't about to give up the search. However, there was still another whole bowl that could dump into the lower half of Rumble Gully and the Ski Patrol weren't about to risk having thirty rescuers buried if it did slide. The skier may have been right near the surface but neither he nor his buddy had transceivers. Without beacons, locating a victim is partly just blind luck. When I found Josh, for example, he was down about as deep as my probe would reach and he was vertical. I must have hit him right on the top of his head. Three inches off, in any direction, and I would have missed. I was also at the far end of the probe line. Basically, your only real chance of surviving an avalanche burial is to have a beacon on.

Later that evening, dogs trained in avalanche rescue and their handlers were flown in from Canada. They had no luck locating the skier either.

So, the skier from this avalanche along with the snowboarder from the January avalanche remained buried where they were. Officially they were listed as missing.

After this avalanche, Mt. Baker Ski Area enhanced their existing backcountry policy as it pertained to people re-entering the ski area. The policy states that "If you leave the ski area boundary into the backcountry or re-enter the ski area from the backcountry, you must have all of the following or you will lose your ski privileges: an avalanche transceiver and demonstrated ability to use it; a partner; a shovel; knowledge of the terrain and your route; avalanche knowledge; and knowledge of local avalanche conditions.

Two weeks after the avalanche, people were leaving the ski area and going into the backcountry, riding over the dead bodies in Rumble Gully.

The autopsy on Josh Adams revealed that the young man suffocated to death. Josh's father Mike was quoted in the Bellingham Newspaper, "It looked safe enough. Everyone had gone through there."

This rescuer stands in the hole to show the depth of burial.

Chapter 3
Reducing the Risk -
Key Points

Before You Go

Get current weather and avalanche information (Appendix E).

Select an area that includes some non-avalanche terrain—especially if the avalanche danger is considerable or higher. If you select an area where most routes and slopes are exposed to avalanches, you have reduced your options and increased the avalanche risk before you have left the house.

Select riders who:

- choose a level of risk you are comfortable with,
- are equipped with avalanche transceivers, probes and shovels,
- know how to use their rescue gear, and
- if possible, know the area and the avalanche slopes in the area.

Check that your avalanche transceivers are working wherever you gear up, preferably before you get to the trailhead, and again when you set off.

On the Way to the Backcountry

Watch for:

- recent avalanches on the slopes above the road, and
- snowfall, rain, blowing snow or warming temperatures.

Some Signs to Watch for in the Backcountry

If you see fresh avalanches or sudden cracks that shoot across the snow, or hear "whumpf" sounds, the avalanche danger is usually *high* or *extreme*. Also, the avalanche danger is probably increasing if you see:

- heavy snowfall,
- rain,
- blowing snow,
- marked warming, or
- warming to the melting point.

Choosing Routes and Slopes

Discuss the route and slopes with the group, considering all the important information. Include less skilled riders in the discussion since they may be good at assessing the avalanche danger and, if not, will learn from the discussion.

Neil Brown photo. Rider Bjorn Lienes.

Avalanches usually start on slopes over 35°, rarely on slopes under 25°.

Windward slopes (that face the recent wind) are usually safer than leeward slopes that face down-wind and collect more snow. Cornices sometimes form at the top of leeward slopes.

If one slope has avalanched recently, others that face the same way are often unstable.

Slopes receiving intense sun, especially in the spring, may be unstable.

Terrain traps increase the danger of particular slopes. They include depressions or creeks in which you might get buried deeply, or cliffs that you might get carried over.

Good Riding Habits

If you think a slope or route is too dangerous, avoid it if possible, or go one at a time.

Watch your fellow riders while they are riding on, or below, an avalanche slope.

Don't stop in areas exposed to avalanches, even to watch a spectacular run or big air.

Most good slopes for free-riding are avalanche slopes. If you decide to go, ride one at a time.

If an avalanche approaches, try to ride to either side, out of its path. If you are about to get caught, release both bindings, if practical.

If you are caught in an avalanche, try to grab trees or rocks. Fight to get to the side of the avalanche, or struggle to stay on the surface of the avalanche.

If you are going to get buried, use one or both hands to make an air space in front of your face when the avalanche slows.

Rescue

Ensure the safety of the remaining members of the group.

Pick a leader.

Switch all transceivers to receive.

Focus the search below the point where the victim was last seen.

Search the avalanche deposit visually for hands, gloves, boots, etc., then search with transceivers for completely buried victims.

When a transceiver searcher is as close to the victim as practical, probe the victim. Leave the probe in place and start shoveling.

Start first aid as soon as the victim's face is exposed.

***

These are the basic steps to reducing the risk. The following chapters of this book cover avalanches, the snowpack and terrain, as well as going into more detail on recognizing avalanche danger and reducing avalanche risk.

Neil Brown photo. Rider Antonin Leiutaghi.

Chapter 4
Avalanche Characteristics

Avalanches range in size from small *sluffs* that would not harm a person to large slides capable of destroying villages and forests. Sometimes considerable quantities of mud, rock or timber are carried within an avalanche.

Types of Avalanches

Avalanches release from snow slopes in two distinct ways. A **point release** or **loose snow avalanche** starts when a small amount of loose snow—typically the size of a snowball—slips and begins to slide down a slope setting additional snow in motion.

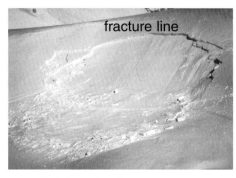

A small slab avalanche.

Alternatively, a **slab avalanche** occurs when a plate or slab of cohesive snow begins to slide as a unit before breaking up. Following a slab avalanche, a distinct fracture line or crown fracture is visible at the top of the slide. Slab avalanches, which are a greater hazard to riders and other recreationists, require that one or more layers of cohesive (strong) snow lie on top of a weak layer. The fractures that release a slab avalanche start in the weak layer. However, some weak layers are difficult to find in the snowpack.

A loose snow avalanche.

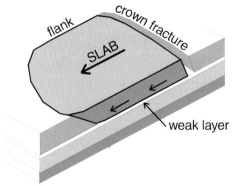

There are few hard-and-fast rules when dealing with avalanche characteristics. However, the following generalizations are useful:

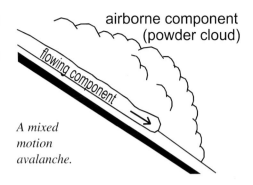

A mixed motion avalanche.

- Slab avalanches are usually larger, more destructive and more difficult to predict than loose snow avalanches.

- Since fractures can spread along weak layers, slab avalanches can be triggered by people who are **not** in the start zone of the avalanche.

- Avalanches involving harder, thicker slabs are generally less predictable[1] and larger[2] than avalanches involving thinner, softer slabs.

Triggers

Most avalanches are triggered when slopes are loaded by additional snow. **However, the majority of avalanches that injure or bury people are triggered by people[3], often by the victim or by a member of the same group[4].** Slabs are triggered when the stress caused by the slab and rider, etc. exceeds the strength of a weak layer in the snowpack.

Natural Triggers

- loading of slope by snowfall
- loading of slope by wind-deposited snow
- warming temperatures or rain
- cornice fall
- clumps of snow falling off trees, rockfall, etc.

Artificial Triggers

- riders, skiers, etc. moving on or near the slope
- explosives

Avalanche Motion and Forces

- Avalanche speeds range widely. Typically, dry slides can attain speeds of 50 to 200 km/h (30 to 120 mph) and wet slides, although usually slower, can attain speeds of 20 to 100 km/h[5] (12 to 60 mph).

- Most avalanches have a flowing component which consists of relatively dense snow flowing down the slope.

- When dry flowing avalanches exceed about 35 km/h (22 mph), a dust or powder cloud of airborne particles of snow moves above the flowing component[5].

- Forces are generally greatest in the flowing component of an avalanche near the ground[5].

- Dry snow avalanches are usually faster than wet snow avalanches[5].

- Most wet snow avalanches have little or no airborne component[6].

- Small wet avalanches can be surprisingly powerful and harmful.

Once they pick up speed, many avalanches are too fast to be outrun by a snowboarder.

This avalanche has just started and the snowboarders have a chance to ride out of its way. Note the slab is breaking up and the dense flowing motion is starting at the tip of the avalanche. John Buffery photo. Riders Tex Davenport and Craig Kelly.

The powder cloud in this mixed motion avalanche hides the denser flowing component. The avalanche is going much too fast to be outrun by snowboarders.

Chapter 5
Avalanche Terrain

Recognizing Avalanche Terrain

The avalanche danger, as reported in public bulletins, is usually not low. Often, we have to select routes and slopes that are appropriate for the current conditions. This requires that we recognize avalanche terrain and the factors that affect the avalanche danger on particular slopes.

The classic avalanche path consists of a starting zone at the top of the path, followed by a narrower track down the slope with a less steep runout zone at the bottom of the path. The starting zone is often steeper than the track and may be shaped or oriented so that it tends to accumulate wind-deposited snow.

Confined avalanche paths are easily recognized as an opening down through trees or between the walls of a gully. Other avalanche slopes, such as the ones on the front and back covers of this book, are not so easily recognized. When on or below slopes steep enough to produce avalanches, look for evidence of avalanches such as:

- fracture lines or avalanche deposits, or
- missing trees, broken-off trees, or trees with missing or broken branches.

Large avalanches have run over this knoll, damaging the trees.

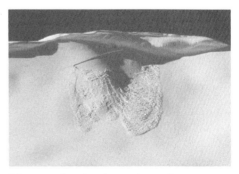

Many avalanche slopes do not have an obvious start zone, track and runout. They are simply steep or moderately steep slopes with few or no trees.

Many open slopes, bowls, chutes and sparsely treed slopes are capable of producing avalanches—under certain conditions.

Slope Angle of the Start Zone

Most avalanches that begin on slopes steeper than 60° are small, loose snow sluffs. Although they are usually small, these avalanches sometimes trigger larger slides on the slopes below.

Larger avalanches usually start on slopes between 30° and 60°. Most large slab avalanches begin on slopes between 30° and 45°. Less than 5% of slab avalanches[7] begin on slopes of less than 30°. Avalanches that *begin* on slopes of less than 25° usually consist of wet snow[8]. Since we are not very good at judging slope angles "by eye" we should use a small lightweight clinometer whenever we are not sure if a slope is steep enough to produce avalanches.

Perhaps the simplest way to avoid avalanches is by not traveling *on or below* slopes steeper than 25° to 30° when the snow is dry. However, this excludes too many fine routes and slopes for most riders. Most of us want to ride slopes over 30°. Reducing the risk on such terrain requires a careful consideration of the avalanche danger (Chapter 7) and safety measures (Chapter 8).

Wind blows up the windward slope removing snow and down the lee slope depositing the snow. The smooth wind-deposited snow on the lee slopes can remain unstable for days.

Orientation of Slope to Wind

Moderate and strong winds will distribute falling snow and redistribute loose snow from previous storms unevenly. Windward slopes (facing the wind) will receive less snow and may be left with a *scoured* appearance. Additional snow will be deposited on lee slopes (facing down-wind). This wind deposit may be pillow-shaped or chalky in appearance. Drifts called cornices sometimes form at the top of lee slopes.

These wind deposits on lee slopes are very important for two reasons:

• Snow will be deposited at several times the overall snowfall rate, which often overloads the buried weak layers and increases the likelihood of avalanches.

• The wind-packed layers have the potential to release as slab avalanches which can be large and triggered from below.

> More slab avalanches occur on lee slopes than windward slopes. Many people have been killed on lee slopes because they did not recognize or under-estimated wind loading of lee slopes.

Snow conditions and avalanche danger are often quite different on the sunny and shady slopes.

Orientation to Sun

Sunny slopes

On sunny days, or days with only thin clouds, snow on south-facing or sunny slopes will warm and weaken faster than snow on shady slopes. Consequently, sunny slopes are more likely to produce avalanches in warm spring-like conditions.

Shady slopes

After storms, the new snow layers tend to remain unstable longer on shady and north-facing slopes than on sunny and south-facing slopes. This is because the snow on these shady slopes settles (and stabilizes) more slowly and because cool shady conditions favor the development of weak layers within the snowpack. Consequently, shady slopes are more likely to produce

avalanches during or following cold, winter-like conditions.

Elevation

Typically, the avalanche danger is higher at higher elevations because there is more snowfall and more wind than at lower elevations. Also, at higher elevations there are fewer trees and bushes that tend to anchor the

Snow conditions will vary from the lower slopes at treeline to the upper slopes near the ridge. Often the snow is less stable above treeline than below.

snowpack (but do not necessarily prevent avalanches). This increase in the avalanche danger with elevation presents a problem since riders usually approach avalanche terrain from lower elevations. Climbing routes should be chosen to reduce the risk. Also, once above treeline, the avalanche danger should be reassessed.

Size of Slope

Clearly, larger slopes can produce larger avalanches. However, there have been a number of serious incidents on small slopes. So, to reduce the risk on small slopes, the avalanche danger should also be assessed (Chapter 7), or the slope avoided. Crossing quickly below small slopes will also help reduce the risk.

Even small slopes can produce serious avalanches. A rider triggered this avalanche and was almost completely buried by it. Fortunately, his head was out of the snow. A skier in the group traversed over and dug out the rider. (The arrow points to the hole.) Note that wind blowing from left to right has deposited pillows at the top of the short slope.

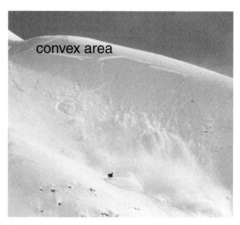

The upper part of this slope is convex—it gets steeper as you descend. Soft slabs like this one are often easily triggered at or just below the convexity. John Buffery photo.

Shape of Slope

The shape of slopes can help us choose our routes. If the slope gets steeper as you descend, it is convex. A concave slope gets less steep as you descend. Snow slopes below cliffs are often concave. When the snow is stable, there is good riding on both convex and concave slopes. A single run often includes both convex and concave slopes.

If you are uncomfortable with the avalanche danger on a particular slope, find a route around it. However, if circumstances require that you cross such a slope, the shape of the slope can help you select your route across it.

Unstable soft slabs are often triggered at or just below the convex part of the slope. If the avalanche danger is a concern, you should cross the top of slope above the convex region. For this reason, benches are often part of good routes.

The safest place to cross a concave slope is often at the top. A rider is more likely to trigger an avalanche from high on a concave slope than from a lower position. However, should a slide occur, a rider caught low on the slope is more likely to be injured or buried than one caught near the top.

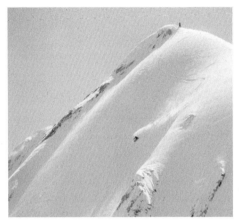

*Gullies are very dangerous places to get caught. It is a good idea to avoid gullies unless you are **sure** the snow is stable. These snowboarders will ride the gully one at a time. John Buffery photo. Riders Craig Kelly and Jason Ford.*

Gullies and Bowls

Bowls and sometimes gullies may offer good boarding when the avalanche danger is low. However, they are generally more dangerous than neighboring slopes for several reasons:

- In gullies and small bowls, there is usually no route to escape from an approaching avalanche.

- Riders caught in a gully by an avalanche will get pushed into the centre of the gully where the forces are highest and a deep burial is likely.

- A gully or the sides of a bowl may be loaded with snow by wind from any one of *several different directions.*

- Even if one side of a bowl has stable snow or has avalanched, travel in the bowl may not be safe because the snow on other sides of the bowl may be unstable.

- The fairly rapid effect of sun-warming, or the long-term effect of shade may reduce the snow stability on a particular side of a gully or bowl.

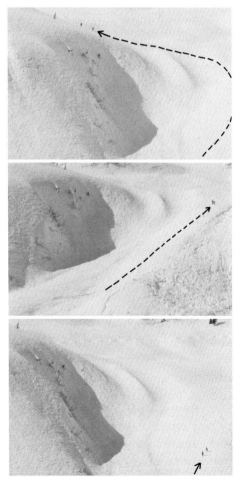

In this sequence, two snowboarders avoid the gully by climbing up to the right of it. It's easier hiking and lower risk.

Terrain Roughness

Bushes and rocks that stick through the snow or cause bumps in the snowpack tend to anchor layers of cohesive snow[8]. However, such a rough ground cover *does not guarantee* that the snow slope will not avalanche. The stabilizing effect of a rough ground cover is lost when additional snow has smoothed over the bumps from rocks and bushes. Also, loose snow avalanches may occur when the bumps, rocks and bushes are still apparent.

While hiking up or riding down this slope, the groups of trees and rock outcrops provide some low risk places to stop and regroup.

Slab avalanches can occur where the snowpack is thin if the ground is smooth, as in this photo.

Islands of Safety

Small groups of trees or large rocks that provide limited shelter from avalanches are often called "islands of safety". When crossing a wide slide path, stopping at such islands may be the only practical way one rider can watch others cross more exposed parts of the path.

During this part of the climb, the rider and snowmobiler can easily stay well back from the steeper slopes. Higher up, they may not have this option.

Timber

Although avalanches are less likely to start in dense trees than on open slopes, avalanches can enter and flow through stands of trees. Even in mature timber, riders should be looking for damage to vegetation and other evidence of avalanches.

Terrain traps such as gullies, cliffs and crevasses increase the chance of injury or burial to a rider, even in a small slide. This glaciated slope has many terrain traps.

Avalanches don't often start in mature forests, but if they start above the forest, they can run through it, often removing the lower branches from trees. The avalanche in this photo ran through the forest and down the adjacent open slope.

Terrain Traps

About 25% of avalanche fatalities are caused by physical injuries[9]. A terrain trap is any terrain feature that makes injuries or burial more likely, or makes escape from an approaching avalanche more difficult. In other words, a small avalanche combined with a terrain trap can have the same effect as a large avalanche. Terrain traps include:

- gullies, cliffs and crevasses since they make escape more difficult and because they concentrate the forces on the victim,

- flats at the bottom of steep slopes that may accumulate a deep avalanche deposit on top of an avalanche victim, and

- trees and large rocks in slide paths since they are likely to cause physical injuries to persons caught in the avalanche.

Route Selection

The following factors are helpful in selecting good routes:

- Wind-scoured slopes are generally safer than wind-loaded slopes.

- Broad valley bottoms are usually safer than the surrounding slopes; but keep in mind that large avalanches can run well across valley bottoms and sometimes start up the other side of the valley.

- Narrow ridges are usually safe from avalanches but there may be a hazard from wind, cornices or the steep slopes beside the ridge.

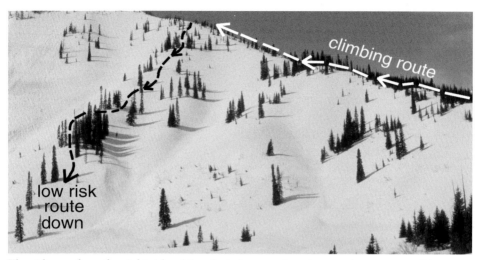

The ridge up from the right side of the photo is a good route up under most conditions. The best run down will depend on conditions but the dashed line shows a low risk route down a broad ridge that avoids two gullies on either side. The broad ridge in the middle of the photo also offers a route that is lower risk than the adjacent gullies.

- Where practical, use benches and avoid steep slopes.

- If there is no way to avoid a slope of doubtful stability, it should be crossed as high as possible.

- In particular, convex portions of slopes should be avoided if you are concerned about the avalanche danger.

- Dense timber is usually considered safe[11] but riding in dense timber is rarely as good as on open slopes.

Although this list of route-finding basics is a useful start, we continue to learn the many subtleties of route selection as long as we ride in the mountains. Traveling with experienced riders is a great way to hone route-finding skills, especially if route selection is discussed within the group.

Terrain Summary

The three main terrain factors that affect avalanche danger are: slope angle, orientation to wind, and terrain traps.

Most dry slab avalanches start on slopes over 30°, especially over 35°.

Unstable wind slabs often form on the down-wind (lee) side of ridges, so windward slopes are often safer than leeward slopes.

Getting caught in a terrain trap such as a gully, or getting carried into one, reduces your chance of survival.

The wind often deposits unstable snow slabs on lee slopes. Failing to recognize or under-estimating wind loading of lee slopes has contributed to many avalanche accidents[10].

Avalanches may be triggered—unexpectedly—from the particularly weak snow next to rocks or bushes. Clearly, such features are not islands of safety[10].

A ridge like this one is a low risk ascent route that allows these riders to climb together.
Dan Hudson photo. Snowboarders Hugh Fraser, Dan Grey and Jonaven Moore.

The left ridge offers a low risk ascent route, but how far up you follow this ridge depends
on the conditions on the slope above. You could ride down the ridge, but the broad gully
*in the middle of the photo offers better riding **if you decide that avalanches are unlikely**.*
There are few trees in the broad gully because it is an avalanche path.

*The broad ridge offers an efficient and low risk ascent route. You could ride down the gentle terrain to the right of the arrows under most conditions. However, the steeper run down to the left of the arrows and the two dark shadows offers better riding **only if you decide that medium or large avalanches are unlikely**. You might decide that the risk due to small avalanches in this terrain would be acceptable. Note the slab avalanche on the left side of the photo. Is it fresh? If so, today may be the wrong day for the route to the left of the arrows.*

Dan Hudson photo. Snowboarder Jonaven Moore.
On the sleds: Justin Baun and Kyle Wolochatiuk.

Chapter 6
Mountain Snowpack

For a slab avalanche, we need a weak layer underneath one or more layers of snow that are more cohesive or stronger than the weak layer. This chapter begins by considering the formation of cohesive (strong) and weak layers within the snowpack, so that we know where to look for slab conditions, i.e. for strong snow on top of a weak layer. The latter part of this chapter outlines how recent weather can increase or decrease the snow stability.

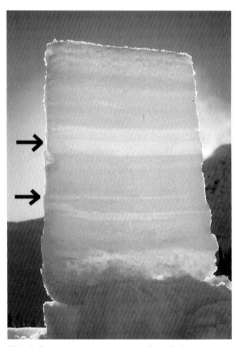

Weak layers are necessary for slab avalanches. This photo shows both thick and thin weak layers (lighter color). Jim Bay photo.

The Strength of Storm Snow Layers

Layers of newly fallen snow vary in strength. Strong layers of new snow often consist of:

- wind-packed snow,
- dense snow, or
- snow that was deposited near 0°C (32°F).

Weak layers of new snow often consist of:

- dry snow deposited without wind, or
- large unbroken star-shaped crystals, or crystals shaped like needles or plates.

The Strength of Old Snow Layers

After new snow crystals have been on the ground for a period of days, they change, or metamorphose into grains of old snow. Corresponding to these changes in grain shape and size, layers of snow either increase or decrease in strength.

Being able to find strong and weak snow layers in the field is essential to assessing snow stability. Understanding how strong and weak layers are formed is much less important and is summarized in Appendix B.

The following factors have the greatest effect on the strength of snow layers:

Load

The more snow on top of a layer, the more the layer tends to strengthen. For this reason, deeply buried weak layers *eventually* gain strength and stabilize.

Snowpack thickness and air temperature

A thick snowpack and mild air temperature favor strengthening of snowpack layers (Appendix B). Hence, weak layers often stabilize faster in the spring.

> A **thin** weak layer of sugar-like crystals called facets, which sometimes forms just above or below a crust, may be more sensitive to triggers than a thicker and easier-to-find weak layer such as depth hoar.

Also, a thin snowpack and cold temperatures often promote weakening of snowpack layers by faceting (Appendix B). Where the snowpack is thin, say less than a metre (3'), a week of cold temperatures may weaken snow layers noticeably. The resulting layers of faceted crystals or depth hoar (Appendix B) may remain weak for a month or more. Once buried by the next snowfall, slab avalanches may slide on weak layers of faceted crystals or depth hoar.

Warming, melting and freezing

When snow layers warm to near 0°C (32°F), they weaken.

At 0°C (32°F), snow may be moist or wet, and the wetter it is, the weaker it is.

When wet snow freezes, it becomes a relatively strong crust. During spring days, the surface of the crust often thaws into corn snow which makes good riding. When the whole crust thaws, it becomes weak and the snowpack may become less stable.

Surface Hoar

If the sky is relatively clear and the wind is light, it only takes one or two cool nights to form a beautiful layer of sparkling frost called surface hoar (or hoarfrost) on top of the snowpack.

Large surface hoar crystals on tree and snow surface. Once buried, surface hoar layers often remain unstable for several weeks.

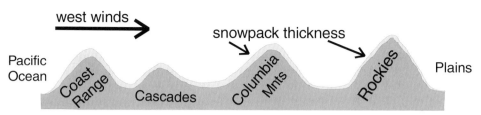

Snowfall decreases from west to east as moist winds off the Pacific Ocean lose their moisture. In the US, the mountains west of the Rockies are called the Intermountain ranges.

When the surface hoar is buried by subsequent snowfalls, it will form a weak layer that can reduce snow stability for weeks, and sometimes a month or more. Surface hoar layers are often thin and difficult to find in the snowpack.

> In the Interior Ranges of BC, many fatal avalanches have started in weak layers of buried surface hoar[12].

Regional Differences in Snowpack

In the mountains of Canada and the United States west of the Rockies, the snowpack is generally thicker and the air somewhat milder than in the Rockies. This effect of snowpack thickness and temperature can be understood by comparing the layering common to thick and thin snowpacks.

West of the Rockies, the thickness of the snowpack and the generally warmer temperatures will cause most layers to become dense and strong over time. During early and mid-winter in the Rockies when the snowpack is usually thin and the air cold, weak layers of faceted grains often form near the surface of the snowpack. Also, a weak layer of relatively large crystals called depth hoar may develop next to the ground.

Local Differences in Snowpack

Anywhere the snowpack is thin—near a ridgetop or over a rock outcrop or bush—the snowpack may be weakened by faceting. Consequently, we sometimes break deeply into weak snow near a buried rock or bush.

Although we can never anticipate every hidden weak spot in the snowpack, we should "think terrain" and try to avoid weak spots. Not only is it tiring to get up out of weak snow, but the fractures that release slab avalanches are sometimes triggered in these hidden weak spots.

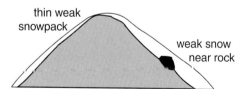

The snow is likely weak where the snowpack is thin near the ridge and over the rock. The snowpack is thicker on the right side of the ridge probably because the wind has blown snow from the left (windward) slope to the right (lee) slope.

Effect of Recent Weather on Snow Stability

Weather factors that decrease snow stability

- snowing hard—more than 2 cm (1") per hour—for a few hours

- rain

- moderate or strong winds (with noticeable drifting)

- rapid warming of snowpack by solar radiation, warm wind or rain

- warming of snow to 0°C (32°F)

- 20 cm (8") or more of snow within the last few days.

Weather factors that tend to increase snow stability

- cooling trend, especially after a thaw

- several days of moderate temperatures that allow the snow from the most recent storm to settle and strengthen.

Dan Hudson photo. Riders Candice Drouin and Kyle Wolochatiuk enjoying near perfect powder on a settled snowpack in the backcountry.

Chapter 7
Recognizing Avalanche Danger

Avalanche Danger

The avalanche danger depends on terrain, snow stability and people. If the snow is unstable and there are no people in avalanche terrain, there may be avalanches but there is no danger to people. If the people are in avalanche terrain but the snow is stable, again they are not in danger.

Since much of the good snowboarding is in avalanche terrain, avalanche danger often depends on snow stability. However, we can use the terrain by selecting smart routes to reduce the danger.

John Buffery photo. Rider Jason Ford.

Making a Decision

For low risk riding, we need to pick routes and lines that suit the current conditions. This process is based on the following three questions:

1. Is the terrain prone to avalanches?

• Much of the good riding is in avalanche terrain.

• If the slope is steep enough for avalanches to start, or if there are signs such as damaged vegetation or lack of trees that suggest that avalanches can run onto the slope, then snow stability must be considered:

2. Is the snow stable?

• This is often the most difficult question and the focus of the rest of this chapter.

• If the snow stability is not good or is in doubt, then your next question is:

Fresh avalanches are the strongest sign of unstable snow. Even a much smaller slide should cause you to re-assess the avalanche danger.

Always look for avalanches. Fresh avalanches usually indicate high avalanche danger. While the absence of recent avalanches is often a good sign, it may not indicate low danger. Other observations and tests must be used.

3. What are the consequences of getting caught by an avalanche on this slope?

- If an avalanche on this terrain could injure or bury a rider, the risk is too high for most riders. Sometimes there are safe routes around unstable slopes. Other times the only safe alternative is to turn around and come back another day when the conditions are better.

- If the only possibility is a small slide on a small slope without terrain traps, the risk may be acceptable to some riders. The precautions outlined in Chapter 8 should be taken to minimize the risk.

Recognition of avalanche terrain and terrain traps is outlined in Chapter 5.

This chapter focuses on Question 2: "*Is the snow stable?*". The best answer to this question is rarely a simple yes or no. In fact, the agencies that provide avalanche information usually rate the avalanche danger in five levels as described in Appendix C. We should use our assessment of snow stability along with our answers to Questions 1 and 3 to decide whether or not to proceed onto a particular slope.

The following sources of information help when assessing snow stability:

- snowpack and previous weather
- public avalanche information
- field observations
- field tests
- present weather.

Snowpack and Previous Weather

The snowpack is a record of the winter's weather. For example, major snowstorms result in thick layers; thaws and rainstorms result in moist layers or crusts; and periods of cold, clear weather sometimes result in layers of surface hoar or a snow layer weakened by faceting (Appendix B).

Before starting a trip, ask locals and the staff at information centers about previous weather and the snowpack (and terrain). For example, reports of a buried layer of surface hoar, or slab avalanches occurring many days after a storm, indicate that a persistent weak layer exists in the snowpack.

> Riders with limited experience assessing snow stability should select terrain with extra caution.

Cornices and wind ribs like this one point toward wind-loaded slopes. When freshly loaded, such slopes are often unstable. Dan Hudson photo. Snowboarder Matt Goodwill.

Avalanche Bulletins

Avalanche bulletins are available for many mountain areas (Appendix E). Sources include recorded telephone messages, and various web sites. Sometimes this information is available in newspapers, or on the radio or TV. Before traveling in or near an area for which public avalanche information is available, the information should be obtained and discussed among the group. Bulletins for the local area are often more useful than bulletins for the entire mountain range.

Most avalanche information agencies rate the avalanche danger using five levels: *low, moderate, considerable, high* or *extreme* (Appendix C).

Field Observations

While on the way to the mountains and while climbing, look for the following:

Avalanches

Note the direction the slope faces (the aspect) and elevation of any fracture lines or avalanche deposits and estimate how long ago they occurred.

Effects of wind

- Drifts, cornices or smooth pillows of snow indicate where snow has been deposited.

- Wind scouring (or sastrugi), usually on the windward slopes and ridge tops, indicates where the wind has picked up snow.

- Rime (which looks like stiff white icing) forms mainly on the windward side of trees, rock outcrops, posts and buildings.

- Clumps of snow that have fallen from trees indicate there has been wind or warming since the last snow storm.

The snowfall is accumulating rapidly on these packs. If the snow continues to fall at this rate, the avalanche danger will increase. Riding without packs is best reserved for non-avalanche terrain.

Wind from the left is depositing snow on the slope. The avalanche danger is increasing quickly.

Wind blowing from left to right has cross-loaded the slope by removing snow from the ribs and deposited snow in the gullies. Cross-loaded slopes are tricky to assess because the snow thickness and stability varies across the slope.

Recent snowfall

Note accumulations of snow on parked cars, snowmobiles, roads, trees, etc.

- 2 cm (1") or more per hour for a few hours will decrease snow stability substantially.

- Snowfalls of 20 cm (8") or more often require a few days to stabilize—longer if the new snow bonded poorly to the old snow, or if the air temperature has been cold.

Rain

- Rain reduces stability by adding weight to the snowpack and weakening surface layers quickly.

Air temperature

- Sudden warming within several hours will reduce snow stability.

- Natural snowballs rolling down slopes indicate that surface layers are warm and weak.

- Snow becoming sticky indicates warming of snow to 0°C (32°F) and weakening of surface layers.

These settlement cracks form gradually around trees and indicate that the recent snow is gaining strength—but deeper weak layers may persist.

- Cracks that open gradually in the snow around trees indicate settlement and strengthening of surface layers over time.

- Following mild temperatures, say -5°C (23°F) or above, a cooling trend will usually improve snow stability.

These pinwheels happen on warm days when the fresh snow surface is moist. Wet snow avalanches can happen under these same conditions. If you only see pinwheels from a few days ago then the snow surface has gained strength.

Effects of hiking and riding on snow

- Sudden collapses (whumphs) or sudden cracking of the snowpack indicate unstable slab conditions.

- Snow beside board tracks and between footprints that breaks up in blocks indicates that surface layers are cohesive and "slabby".

- Deep footprints and board tracks indicate considerable soft snow is available for wind loading. Also, if avalanches start, they will likely become large when deep loose snow in the path is set in motion.

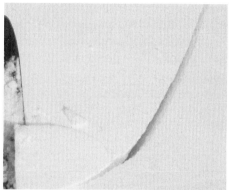

Shooting cracks like this or whumpf sounds indicate that there is an unstable slab and that snowboarders can trigger the slab.

Control activity for ski areas or highways

- Avalanche closures or blasting generally indicate unstable snow in the area.

If you need more information about the snowpack, pick a site for a profile and snowpack tests that is relatively safe, undisturbed and representative of the slopes you want to ride. John Buffery photo. Riders Craig Kelly and Tex Davenport.

Field Tests

While in or near avalanche terrain, observations should be complemented by field tests of the snowpack. Before stopping to do a field test, ask yourself the following questions:

1. Is this a safe location? Remember that some of the tests, such as a test profile, may take 10 or more minutes.

2. Is the snow at this location disturbed by avalanches, snowboard, snowshoe or snowmobile tracks, drifting around trees, clumps of snow that have fallen off trees, etc.? Undisturbed sites provide better information.

3. How well does this location represent the slopes you want to ascend, descend or cross?

Some of the more useful field tests are on the following pages:

Test profile

A test profile is an observation of snow layers from a pit dug in the snowpack.

Probing the site will help determine if there are bushes or large rocks which might make the profile misleading. A profile in a safe, undisturbed location near the valley bottom will tell you the basic layering in the area so you can test for *changes* in the snowpack as you ascend. At higher elevations where the snowpack may be quite different, additional tests or profiles are often required.

Pits for test profiles should be dug with one smooth wall across the slope and one down the slope. Dig deeper than any suspected weak layers; a metre (3') deep is often, but not always, sufficient. Several quick profiles at different locations usually provide more useful information than one detailed profile.

Looking and feeling for strong and weak layers in a profile.

Some major layers will be visible on the wall of the snow pit. Strong and weak layers can be detected by poking the exposed layers by hand, by brushing, or by sliding a finger, credit card or ruler up and down through the layers and noting the changes in resistance. A compression or shovel shear test is often the final part of a test profile.

Shovel tilt test (burp test)

To test for weak layers near the top of the snowpack, cut a square column with sides about 30 cm (12") wide. Pick up the top 30-40 cm (12-16") of the column on your shovel, tilt the shovel blade to about 15° and tap the bottom of the shovel with your hand, gently at first, then harder. Weak layers within the snow block will show up as smooth fractures.

By tapping on the bottom of the shovel, the burp test can find most weak layers in the top 30 cm of the snowpack.

We should be a bit skeptical when interpreting field tests since they over-estimate the stability **at least** 10% of the time[13-16].

Compression test (tap test)[13, 17]

The compression test finds most unstable layers in the upper part of the snowpack and rates their stability. Weak layers are identified when they compress and show up on the walls of the snow column. To start this test, use a shovel, snow saw or snowboard to cut a square column with sides 30 cm (12") wide. The column is usually about 1 m (3') tall.

These compressive fractures are rated according to the force required. *Very easy* means the layer failed when you cut the column. Next, place a shovel blade on top of the column. Tap with finger tips, moving your hand from the wrist; rate any failure as *easy*. Tap from the elbow, and rate any failure as *moderate*. Finally hit the shovel blade with an open hand or fist and rate any failures as *hard*.

By tapping on top of the column with increasing force, the compression test can find many of the weak layers that concern riders, and give an indication of stability.

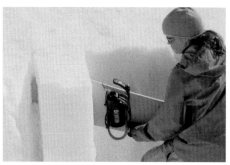

Your board works well for cutting columns for the compression and shovel test.

Shovel shear test[17]

This test can be done on the flats or on a slope. With good technique, the location of weak layers—even thin weak layers—can usually be found. To start, cut the front wall and two sides of a 30 cm (12") square column. Cut the back of the column *only* about 5-10 cm (2-4") below a suspected weak layer and make the cut wide enough for the shovel blade. Place the shovel behind the column and down almost as

For the shovel shear test, the back wall should not be cut more than 15 cm below the suspected weak layer.

far as the suspected weak layer. Use both hands to pull the shovel downslope until a weak layer in the column "shears" (i.e breaks along a smooth plane). Rate the force required to cause the smooth fracture as either *very easy, easy, moderate* or *hard*. Ignore fractures that are not smooth.

To test for deeper weak layers remove the top of the column and cut down the back wall to the next suspected weak layer and repeat the test.

Although the shovel test helps to find weak layers, it gives only a very rough indication of the strength of the weak layer at the test site.

Slope tests

Riders can test short slopes that are steep enough to avalanche—by turning hard near the top of the slope and quickly riding to a safe spot. This gives an indication of the stability of nearby larger slopes. However, even small avalanches on short slopes can injure riders. Consider the consequences of an avalanche when you select a test slope.

Also, avalanches on test slopes are an indication that nearby larger slopes are probably unstable. Unfortunately, if you don't trigger an avalanche on the test slopes, it doesn't mean you cannot trigger a slide on nearby larger slopes. When assessing the avalanche danger, slope tests are only one piece of the puzzle, as discussed in this chapter.

This rider has just cut hard at the top of a small convex roll to try to trigger a slab. He chose a small slope so the consequences of an avalanche would not be serious. A test like this is just one piece of information that helps us assess the avalanche danger. Photo by Selkirk Mountain Experience.

Rutschblock test[14-16,18]

Skiers have used this test for many years. Snowboarders often use a slightly narrrower block, about the length of the board[18].

Select a slope of at least 25° to 45°. Shovel out the bottom wall and both sides of a block about 1.7 m (6') across and 1.5 m (5') down the slope. Cut the upper wall with a cord or your board. Or cut both sides and the upper wall with a cord around probes placed at the top corners.

Cutting the block is considered the first loading stage. For the next stages, the rider:

2. gently steps or slides onto the top of the block

3. pushes down with his or her legs

4. jumps up then lands on the compacted spot

5. repeats the jump

6. hops or slides down almost to the middle of the block and jumps several times.

What do the results say about the stability of nearby slopes with similar conditions? Well, if the block slides before the jumps (loading stage 1, 2 or 3) **you can probably trigger a slab nearby**.

If the block slides on the first two jumps near the top of the block (stage 4 or 5) **you might be able to trigger a slab nearby**. Other information is the key to deciding if or where to ride.

If the block slides only after moving to the middle of the block, or does not slide cleanly, then the risk of triggering is probably low on nearby slopes but you still need to consider other information such as recent avalanches, weak layers evident in the pit wall, windloading or warming.

To do a rutschlock test without digging the side walls, lay a cord around two probes at the top corners of the block. One rider, then the other, pulls his or her end of the cord to "saw" the cord through the snow.

The rider's first jump (stage 4)

Triggers a shallow slab.

The next jump, stage 5, triggers a deeper slab. So this day is a good day to avoid big slopes. Dan Hudson photos.

As with slope tests, if you cannot trigger the block then it may still be possible to trigger an avalanche on nearby slopes. But block tests and/or slope tests can be used with the other factors described in this chapter to continuously assess the avalanche danger.

Present Weather

The weather forecast for the day can be obtained from the newspaper, radio, TV, recorded telephone messages, web sites or information centers. Ask yourself: Will the forecasted weather tend to increase or decrease the avalanche danger?

While riding in the mountains, consider how the actual weather is affecting the avalanche danger and be alert for changes in weather and snow stability.

Assessing Snow Stability

Observations or test results that clearly indicate unstable snow

- avalanche activity on similar slopes

- collapses, whumpf sounds or shooting cracks near the slope, or on similar slopes

- a block test that slides

- two or more *very easy* or *easy* failures (shovel tilt, compression or shovel shear test).

Observations or test results often associated with unstable snow

Precipitation

- 2-3 cm (1") of snow per hour for two or more hours
- 20 cm (8") or more of snow within two days
- rain.

Wind

- recent or current loading of lee slopes.

Temperature

- marked warming
- warming to 0°C (32°F) or above
- no overnight freeze.

Snowpack

- weak layers with *easy* or *moderate* failures (burp, compression or shovel test).

Factors usually associated with stable snow

- a snowpack that has re-frozen after surface layers were wet
- no smooth failures after several careful compression or shovel tests.

Photo by Selkirk Mountain Experience.

Unfortunately, if there is enough snow to slide, there are no conclusive signs of good stability. Also, you should be careful about using the results of such tests for slopes of different aspect, elevation or incline.

In the absence of precipitation, wind loading or deep weak layers, the following factors are usually associated with improving stability:

- obvious cooling trend especially following air temperatures near or above 0°C (32°F), or
- settlement cracks around trees.

Often the snow stability has to be assessed based on a combination of the information, observations and test results mentioned so far in this chapter.

Unfortunately, **there is no simple rule or formula for combining these factors**.

Experience gained from seasons of travel in avalanche terrain and from traveling with knowledgeable riders will help you make sound decisions about snow stability. At the end of this chapter there are three examples of decision-making.

Terrain Alternatives

For low risk snowboarding, most avalanche slopes—especially large avalanche slopes—should be avoided unless the public avalanche bulletin, field observations or field tests indicate that the snow stability is good.

Sometimes, a safe alternate route may require bushwhacking or following a ridge. In some situations, the only safe alternative is to turn around.

Human Factors

Blue sky draws us towards open slopes and high passes. However, a slab can remain unstable for days or sometimes weeks after the last storm. Decisions should be based on avalanche bulletins, field observations, experience and facts, and not on the good feeling of being out with friends on a blue-sky day.

Many snowboarders are goal-oriented. Some get so focused on riding a perfect line or big air, that they continue even after learning of potentially dangerous conditions!

> For many or us, turning around is difficult. However, the snow slopes will still be there next weekend, and next winter.

Some accidents happen late in the day, especially when the weather is poor. Under such conditions, backcountry travelers often become less careful about selecting routes or observing snowpack conditions[19]. Instead, they focus on getting back to the car.

If we find ourselves thinking, "It won't happen to me" or "It's probably okay to cross this slope," our safety margin is too thin. The mountain snowpack continues to surprise even the most experienced riders, skiers and mountaineers. We need a wide margin of safety so we can continue to enjoy the mountains, winter after winter.

Danger Factors Often Neglected

An analysis of accident reports[23] shows that recreationists have repeatedly failed to recognize the hazard due to:

- terrain traps
- wind-deposited snow
- weak layers, including weak layers deep in the snowpack
- sun-warmed slopes
- the possibility of triggering avalanches on the slopes above
- the possibility of a second avalanche on the same slope.

Summary

The questions that help us recognize and avoid avalanche danger are:

1. Is the terrain prone to avalanches?
2. Is the snow stable? This is the most difficult question. We use public avalanche bulletins, field observations and field tests.
3. What are the consequences of getting caught by an avalanche on this terrain?

Dan Hudson photo. Rider Karleen Jeffery.

Decision-Making Example 1

Public Avalanche Bulletin Generally *low* avalanche danger. However, slabs on lee slopes above treeline have been slower to stabilize resulting in *moderate* avalanche danger.

Recent Weather A 30 cm (12") snowfall a week ago was accompanied by moderate southwest winds. Since then winds have been light, temperatures have ranged from -15° to -5°C (5° to 23°F) and the only snowfall has been a few flurries.

Today's Weather The air temperature should rise to -10°C (14°F) during the day. Light west winds and 5 cm (2") of snow are expected.

Field Observations

- a few old fracture lines on north and northeast slopes
- some settlement cracks around trees
- snow depth at treeline is 1.5 m (4')
- snowshoe tracks at treeline are 15 cm (6") deep

Field Tests at Treeline

- compression test: a *hard* failure 20 cm (8") below the surface

Decision Southwest winds loaded lee slopes a week ago. Since then the weather has favored stabilization of the storm snow. The snowfall and west winds forecast for today will have little effect on stability provided the wind and snowfall remain light. The compression test did not find any *easy* or *moderate* failures. All these factors are consistent with the *low* avalanche danger forecast below treeline. With the safety measures described in Chapter 8, we can ride below treeline with limited risk. However, for low-risk riding, those great-looking lee slopes above treeline should either be avoided, or reassessed once we get to them. Snowpack tests such as the compression or shovel test can help us decide whether or not to avoid lee slopes.

In this photo, the rider has triggered the surface snow only! Where there are no weak layers and no terrain traps, the avalanche danger may be low. Photo by Selkirk Mountain Experience.

Decision-Making Example 2

Recent Weather The winter has been generally cold. Six days ago 25 cm (10") of snow fell. Since then the weather has been cold and clear with light winds.

Today's Weather Clear skies, light winds, forecast high of -18°C (0°F).

Information from Locals The locals (who understand avalanche danger) have been avoiding steep slopes and report numerous shooting cracks and whumphs (fractures of buried weak layers).

Field Observations Two slab avalanches apparently ran after or near the end of the storm. One small slab avalanche is visible on a northeast slope just below treeline; another larger slab has released in the alpine on a northwest-facing slope.

Field Tests At treeline, there is 90 cm (3') of snow on the ground. Snowmobile tracks are 30 cm (12") deep. When probed, the bottom 30 cm (12") of the snowpack is noticeably weaker than the middle of the pack.

Decision Because of the cold weather, the stability of the entire snowpack including the storm snow will not be improving. The weak base and the reported collapses indicate riders are likely to trigger slopes that are steep enough to slide. Avalanche terrain should be avoided, both above and below treeline. We should content ourselves with traveling on terrain that is not exposed to any avalanche paths, or seek alternative recreation. The public avalanche bulletin—had we remembered to call for it—reports widespread *high* avalanche danger, with some slides running on the ground.

This rider may have been tripped up by the surface avalanche. However, if there are no terrain traps or extreme terrain and no deeper weak layers, the avalanche danger may be low. However, on an adjacent slope with a terrain trap, the avalanche danger will be higher. Neil Brown photo. Rider Evan Feen.

Decision-Making Example 3

Recent Weather A spring squall deposited 5-10 cm (2-4") in the mountains four days ago. Since then the sky has been clear, with temperatures rising to +5°C (41°F) each day and dropping to -15°C (5°F) each night. Winds have been light.

Today's Weather Sunny, warming to +8°C (46°F), winds light.

Information from Locals Firm corn snow in the morning turns to wet mush in the afternoon.

Field Observations at 10:30 am Noisy wet loose slides starting in east-facing cliff bands. Large snowballs rolled down south-facing slopes, probably yesterday.

Field Tests A compression and a shovel test both found a *hard* failure 40 cm (16") below the surface.

Decision It's springtime! We want to be leaving avalanche terrain before the corn snow that froze last night gets mushy and unstable. The sun will warm and weaken the snow on east-facing slopes first, then south-facing slopes and finally west-facing slopes. The noisy slides from the east-facing cliff bands indicate that we are probably too late for east-facing slopes. We should check south- and west-facing slopes next; hopefully we can get to them, assess their stability and—if conditions are favorable—use them before the snow surface becomes mushy.

Shady and north-facing slopes may not have experienced the same daily melting and freezing of the surface layers. Their stability may be quite different and should be checked out with field tests such as a profile or compression test before we decide whether or not to use them.

Neil Brown photo. On this day rider Antonin Leiutaghi chose to stay away from steep slopes. That has not stopped him from finding some great riding.

Chapter 8
Smart Riding Habits

Safety Equipment

Every rider in avalanche terrain should carry a transceiver, probe and shovel—and know how to use them.

When a rider gets caught in an avalanche, you'll need a transceiver, probe and shovel for an efficient rescue. The shovel can also be used for building kickers or snow shelters. The probe can be used to help assess slab avalanche conditions.

The group should also have:

- repair kit (tools)
- first aid kit
- extra food
- extra warm clothing
- foam pad and bivvy sack (sleeping bag cover)

In remote areas, your group should also carry a map, compass, altimeter and perhaps a GPS receiver. The group should also consider taking a personal locator beacon and a cell phone or field programmable handheld FM radio and a list of frequencies for

In an avalanche, a snowboard acts like an anchor. Current snowboard bindings don't release if you are getting trashed in an avalanche. When you are about to get caught, bending down and releasing **both** bindings is difficult with some bindings and impossible with others. Some riders are improvising quick releases but we have not heard reports of riders releasing their bindings in avalanches.

emergency assistance. Put the emergency frequencies into the radio's memory before the trip.

Appendix H contains a checklist for a one-day trip.

This improvised quick release uses a strap down the side of one leg and a cord between the release levers of the step-in binding. If you improvise a quick release, make sure it works.

Trip Preparation

Route plan

On short day-trips, hazardous terrain can often avoided by returning along the access route. However, for long day-trips and overnight trips, try to plan alternate routes that avoid avalanche terrain and areas such as glaciers and ridge tops which are prone to "whiteouts" and high winds. Obviously, safe places to camp should be planned in advance. Less obviously, be prepared to camp out on a hut-based tour in case one of the huts cannot be found in stormy weather.

These riders are discussing routes with a ski patroler before going out of bounds.

Local information

Ask locals, ski patrollers or guides about access routes, travel conditions, the snowpack, weather trends and avalanche activity. Then go and see for yourself. First-hand information is always better than second-hand information.

Public forecasts and bulletins

Weather and avalanche forecasts are invaluable and can be obtained from the media, recorded telephone messages or the Internet (Appendix E).

Group compatibility

Some snowboarders like soft, open slopes, others prefer pointing it in steep chutes; and still others are looking for the perfect kicker. If riders with these various expectations are mixed in the same group, the group will often split up. It is far better to agree on the pace and expectations when planning the trip. Factors that affect pace include fitness and how you climb: boots, snowshoes or split-board.

Leadership

Many people prefer to travel in groups of peers without a designated leader. In such situations, the entire group should be involved in assessing the avalanche danger and selecting appropriate routes and slopes.

Check that your transceivers can transmit and receive, preferably before you get to the trailhead.

However, in difficult situations such as an avalanche rescue, a group with a leader will function better than a group without a leader. Some good leaders will only take charge in difficult situations.

Group Safety

Give a responsible friend a copy of your trip plan, noting the location you plan to park and your vehicle's license plate number.

Be sure you know who will bring each item of group and safety equipment and then, just before the trip starts, check that no equipment has been forgotten.

Each morning when gearing up, check that your transceivers are working. Once a month or so, check the full transmit and receive range of your transceiver.

It's best to start each day of your trip early and plan to finish early. That way a minor injury or broken board or binding is less likely to require travel after dark.

A surprising number of accidents happen when members of a group get split up and can't see each other.

Placing a strong rider at the back of a large group is one way of keeping the group together.

Sometimes a quiet voice asking, "But why do we think this slope is stable?" can make you review the conditions and ultimately, lead to a sound decision.

This group is picking the best route for current conditions.

Also, people "back in the pack" may just follow the track, paying little attention to the terrain or snowpack.

In a large group, it's a good idea that the strong rider at the back of the group carry a repair kit.

Hiking and Riding in Avalanche Terrain

Even after you have decided to climb up or ride down a particular slope, the following precautions help reduce the avalanche risk:

• Go one at a time.

• Plan your route, your escape route, and who will go first and last.

- When not riding, move to a safe place where you can watch the others in your group.

- Go where the snow is deepest, avoiding areas where the slab may be thin and easily triggered[10].

- In open terrain stay in visual contact. Look back to check that you are not getting too far ahead of the rider behind you.

- In the trees, ride in pairs and call out to stay in voice contact. "Leapfrog" your partner by stopping often, and letting him or her pass you.

Falling headfirst into the hollow of soft snow around a tree (the tree well) **can be deadly.** If you can no longer hear your partner while riding in the trees, stop riding and start searching! If you find your partner in a tree well, jump feet first into the opposite side of the tree well, clear the snow from around their face and start first aid. Remember that his or her head, neck or back may be injured.

Crossing a Possibly Unstable Slope

If possible, find a safer route.

- Choose escape routes before entering the slope.

- Fasten clothing.

- If your pack is large or heavy, undo the waist belt.

If an avalanche approaches, you **may** be able to **point it** and escape the avalanche. However, if you get caught, your board is your worst enemy, dragging you down while you are struggling to stay on top of the flow.

- Travel quickly one at a time between islands of safety. Persons in safe places should observe those exposed to the hazard.

- If an avalanche approaches, call out to observers and try to ride to safety, usually to the side of the avalanche.

If You Can't Ride Out of the Avalanche

- If you can't ride to the side, release both bindings if possible.

- Get rid of your pack if it is large or heavy.

- Swim or struggle to stay on the surface of the avalanche.

- Fight to get towards the side of the avalanche.

- Grab trees, rocks, etc.

- Keep your mouth shut.

When the Avalanche Slows

- Make a strong thrust towards the surface[9].

- Push one arm towards the surface, if you think the surface is near.

- Make an air space in front of your face with your hands, or with one hand if you pushed an arm toward the surface.

When the Avalanche Stops

- Make an initial attempt to dig yourself out.
- Then, if buried, try to relax your breathing and stay calm.
- Shout only when a searcher is near.

Many people are injured or killed in situations they know to be dangerous. We must not let our desire to reach a pass or ride a perfect chute override our assessment of the danger.

Neil Brown photo. Rider Tyler Massey.

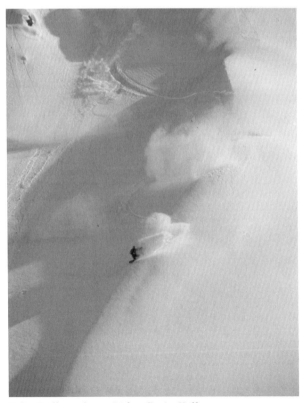

John Buffery photo. Rider Craig Kelly.

Chapter 9
Search and Rescue

Once Buried, Time is Short

Approximately 25% of avalanche victims are fatally injured by the motion of the avalanche or collisions with the ground, trees or rocks[6]. An additional 25% die from suffocation in the next 30 minutes. Therefore, to have a 50% chance of saving a rider who has been buried by an avalanche, that person should be found and dug out within half an hour.

> In most backcountry situations, if you go out to get help from an organized or professional rescue group, there is little chance the buried person(s) will still be alive when the rescue group arrives at the avalanche. Companion rescue is by far the victim's best chance for survival.

Companion Rescue

If you see the avalanche

- Watch the victim and note the last seen point.

Before you enter the slope

- Be calm and methodical.
- Appoint a leader.
- Note who is missing.

- Assess further danger, and post an avalanche guard in a safe place if necessary.

- Ensure everyone knows where to run if another avalanche occurs.

- If your group is large, designate shovelers.

- Leave heavy and unnecessary items away from the search area.

- Designate who will enter the slope and ensure that **all** their transceivers are switched to receive.

> The visual search for surface clues should start **before** the transceiver search or any probing.

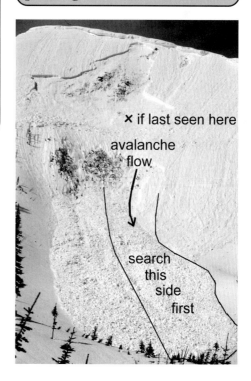

× if last seen here

avalanche flow

search this side first

Look for exposed arms, legs, clothing, gear first—before the transceiver search.

When you Enter the Slope

- If practical, mark the last seen point with a branch, etc.

- Look for the victim's hands, gear, etc. sticking out of the snow; investigate these first, leaving articles in place.

- Focus the initial search on major deposits below the last seen point and in line with the victim's articles.

- Don't leave your helmet, gloves, etc., on the slope.

- Don't spit or urinate on the slope. (Either could subsequently distract an avalanche dog.)

Transceiver Search

A transceiver search is appropriate if at least one searcher and one buried victim have transceivers.

- Switch your transceiver to receive. Set the volume to maximum.

- Select a coarse search pattern and a number of transceiver-searchers that suit the size of slope and the deposits.

- When you pick up a signal, call out "Signal" to let the other searchers know you are leaving the coarse search and starting the fine search. Use either the "induction line"

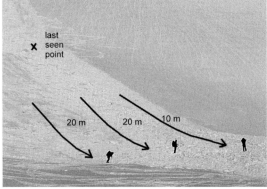

When several searchers are trying to pick up a transceiver signal, they should start 20 m (60′) apart and 10 m (30′) from the side of the deposit.

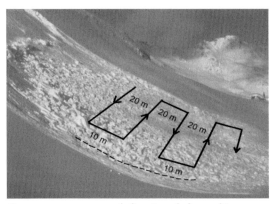

One person can search for signals by making traverses 20 m (60′) apart and 10 m (30′) from the edge of the deposit. James Blench photo.

method or "bracketing" method described in the next section.

- Gently probe the victim and leave the probe in place while shoveling.

- Give the victim first aid and turn their transceiver to receive if additional avalanches are unlikely.

- When the last victim is uncovered, turn all transceivers to transmit.

- If your group has a radio or cell phone and you require help to evacuate the victim, call for assistance.

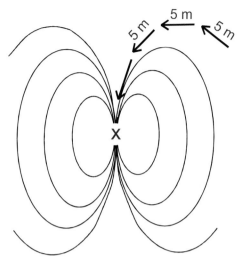

The induction line method is usually faster since it involves less walking on the avalanche deposit.

Move quickly over the deposit and home in on the victim's signal.

Fine Search Patterns for Transceivers

There are two different patterns for the fine search: induction line and bracketing. The induction line method is only recommended for the single frequency 457 kHz transceivers. Both methods finish with the same final search technique (pin-pointing). These search patterns are best learned in the field.

Induction line (tangent method)

1. While holding the transceiver with the arrow pointing ahead of you, turn your body and the transceiver to obtain the maximum volume.

2. If possible, turn down the volume so the beep is quiet but audible.

3. Walk about 5 m (15'). If the signal gets weaker, walk 10 m (30') in the opposite direction.

4. While holding the transceiver in front of you, turn your body for maximum volume. Turn the volume down if practical, and walk 5 m (15') in the direction the transceiver is pointing.

5. Repeat until the signal gets weaker while going ahead or back. Then pin-point the signal with the Final Search Method.

Bracketing (grid search)

1. When you first hear the signal (Point A in the diagram), reorient (R) the transceiver for maximum volume and, if possible, decrease (D) the volume until the beep is still audible. (These two steps are labelled R & D in the diagram).

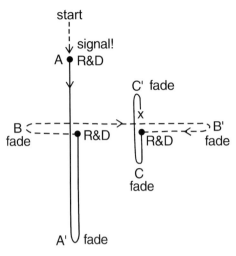

A bracket extends in a straight line between two fade points. After finishing a bracket, return to the middle, reorient the transceiver for maximum volume (R) and decrease the volume (D) if possible before starting the next bracket.

2. While holding the transceiver in the loudest orientation, proceed in the original direction until the signal fades (A'). To complete the A-A' bracket, return to where the signal is strongest, or to the midpoint of the bracket.

3. Reorient (R) the transceiver for maximum volume and, if possible, decrease (D) the volume (R & D in the diagram).

4. Holding the transceiver in this loudest orientation, begin a new bracket (B-B') at 90° to the previous bracket.

5. Each bracket will tend to be shorter than the previous bracket. Continue bracketing at 90° to the previous bracket until you reach the lowest practical volume setting. This leads naturally to the final search pattern (pin-pointing).

Final search (pin-pointing)

1. Loosen the strap or remove the transceiver so you can hold the transceiver close to the snow.

2. Move the transceiver along a straight line (mini-bracket) by moving your feet, instead of just reaching with the transceiver. Pause for each beep so you can compare the loudness of the beeps, until you find the strongest signal along the mini-bracket.

3. From the point with the strongest signal, do another mini-bracket at 90° to the previous one.

*For the pin-point search, hold the transceiver low and find the strongest signal with short brackets, then probe the victim, leave the probe in place and **dig quickly**.*

4. Repeat the mini-brackets until the strongest signal in any direction has been located.

5. Gently probe to locate the person and start shoveling.

Searching for multiple signals

• If you hear more than one signal while searching, turn down your transceiver at every opportunity. This may reduce the number of signals you can hear.

- Each buried transceiver will have distinct patterns of beeps. Focus your attention on one pattern while you search.

- If you appear to be converging on the same signal as another searcher, back away and try to pick up another signal.

Probe Search

Compared to a transceiver search, a probe search is very, very slow. Specially designed probes work best but people have been found by probing with poles and branches.

- If your group has a radio or cell phone, call for help.

- Ensure searchers have their transceivers on transmit.

- Identify likely deposits in line with avalanche flow from the last seen point.

- Spot-probe (without using a line of probers) any small, likely deposits.

- If the spot-probing is unsuccessful, set up a line of probers (or two), again considering the last seen point and estimated trajectory.

Three hole-per-step probing[20, 21]

This new coarse probing technique searches the deposit faster than traditional techniques. Groups of about 5 or 6 probers in a line work best.

- Probers should stand fingertip-to-fingertip apart, about 175 cm (70").

- The probemaster should be on one end of the line, probing with the others and setting a pace that can be maintained.

- The probemaster coordinates the probe line with the commands "Probes down" and "Step forward."

- On the command "Probes down," push the probe down between your feet and remove it. Reach to your left and push the probe, at a slight angle, into the snow 50 cm (20") to the left of the first hole. Repeat 50 cm to the right of the first hole.

- Step forward 70 cm (28").

Spot probe (no line of probers) at likely burial sites such as where clothes or gear are found, or where the deposit is deep.

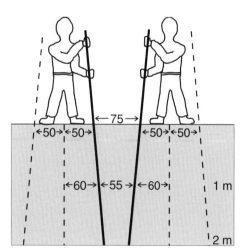

After probing between your feet, to the left and to the right, step forward 70 cm (28"). The probes to the left and right should be close to vertical.

After the visual search, transceiver search and spot probing, probe lines such as this are the next procedure. Lines of 5 or 6 probes are often faster than a single longer line of probers. Rob Orvig photo.

- If your probe encounters any soft or suspicious objects, leave it in the snow. If additional (gentle) probing confirms the possible presence of a victim, then begin shoveling.

- If possible, use flagging or wands to mark probed areas.

- After probing all deposits below the last seen point, either do it again or send for organized help.

Going for Organized Help

- Don't rush off.

- Write the accident situation and the group's needs on paper (Appendix F).

- Mark the accident location, a suitable location for a helicopter to land and a proposed route on a map.

- Plan the trip, and take ample supplies.

- If possible, don't travel alone.

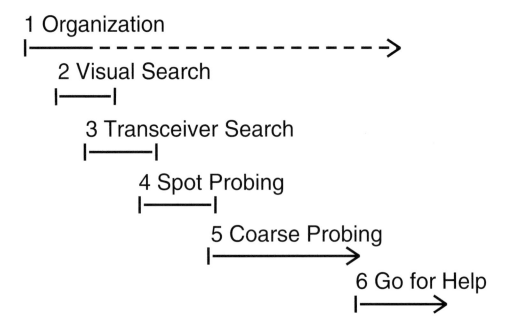

The Stages of Companion Search

1 Organization
|——— – – – – – – – – – – – – – – – – – ->

   2 Visual Search
    |———|

      3 Transceiver Search
       |————|

         4 Spot Probing
          |————|

            5 Coarse Probing
             |—————>

               6 Go for Help
                |————>

Digging, First Aid, Evacuation

Organized Rescue

An organized avalanche rescue party will typically include a helicopter, a trained avalanche dog, advanced first aid equipment and—most importantly—the people trained to use these resources.

Before the helicopter lands, secure light objects, stay well back from the landing site, put on your hat or helmet and lower your goggles. Approach the helicopter only when directed by the pilot and then crouch while approaching from the front (or front downhill side), making sure the pilot can see you.

As a member of the accident party, you should:

- provide information about the accident such as last seen point, number of people missing and type of transceivers used,

- tell the person in charge how you feel (cold, exhausted, etc.),

- assist the rescue team if you are asked.

Only about 25% of buried victims are found alive. The best way not to be found dead is not to get caught, or at least not to get caught in a slide big enough to kill or bury you.

Neil Brown photo. Rider Paul Decarrie.

Dan Hudson photo. Rider Karleen Jeffery.

Neil Brown photo. Riders Sean Johnson and Mike Orr.

Books, Videos and References

Some Good Reading

Books available at most mountain shops:

Snow Sense: A Guide to Evaluating Avalanche Hazards, third edition, by J.A. Fredston and D. Fesler. 1988. (Alaska Mountain Safety Center, Anchorage), 48 pp.

Avalanche Accidents in Canada, Volume 4: 1984-96. B. Jamieson and T. Geldsetzer. 1996. (Canadian Avalanche Association, P.O. Box 2759, Revelstoke, BC, V0E 2S0), 202 pp.

The Snowy Torrents - Avalanche Accidents in the United States 1980-86, by N. Logan and D. Atkins. 1996. (Colorado Geological Survey, Special Publication 39), 275 pp.

Avalanche Safety for Skiers and Climbers, second edition, by T. Daffern. 1992. (Rocky Mountain Books, Calgary), 192 pp.

The Avalanche Handbook, by D.M. McClung and P.A. Schaerer. 1993. (The Mountaineers, Seattle), 271 pp.

The Avalanche Book, revised edition, by B.R. Armstrong and K. Williams. 1992. (Colorado Geological Survey, Denver, CO), 240 pp.

The ABC of Avalanche Safety, second edition, by E.R. LaChapelle. 1985. (The Mountaineers, Seattle), 112 pp.

And Some Videos

Beating the Odds, 30 and 52 minutes. Canadian Avalanche Association, P.O. Box 2759, Revelstoke, BC, V0E 2S0. Phone 1-250-837-2435. http://www.avalanche.ca

Winning the Avalanche Game, 58 minutes. Friends of the Utah Avalanche Forecast Center, Box 521353, Salt Lake City, UT 84152-1353. Phone 1-801-488-1003

References

1. T. Daffern. 1992. Avalanche Safety for Skiers and Climbers, second edition. (Rocky Mountain Books, Calgary), 192 pp.

2. B. Jamieson and C.D. Johnston. 1992. A fracture-arrest model for unconfined dry slab avalanches. Canadian Geotechnical Journal 29, 61-66. Also adapted for Proceedings of the 1990 International Snow Science Workshop, Bigfork, (ISSW '90, P.O. Box 372, Bigfork, MT), 234-244.

3. B. Jamieson and T. Geldsetzer. 1996. Avalanche Accidents in Canada, Vol. 4: 1984-96. (Canadian Avalanche Association, P.O. Box 2759, Revelstoke, BC, V0E 2S0), 202 pp.

4. N. Logan and D. Atkins. 1996. The Snowy Torrents - Avalanche Accidents in the United States 1980-86. (Colorado Geological Survey, Special Publication 39), 275 pp.

5. P.A. Schaerer. 1981. Avalanches in: Handbook of Snow, Eds. D.M. Gray and D.H. Male (Pergamon Press, Toronto), 475-518.

6. D.M. McClung and P.A. Schaerer. 1993. The Avalanche Handbook, second edition. (The Mountaineers, Seattle), 271 pp.

7. R.I. Perla. 1977. Slab avalanche measurements. Canadian Geotechnical Journal 14(2), 206-213.

8. E.R. LaChapelle. 1985. The ABC of Avalanche Safety, second edition, (The Mountaineers, Seattle), 112 pp.

9. P.A. Schaerer. 1988. Studies on survival in avalanches. Canadian Alpine Journal 71, 55-56.

10. N. Logan. 1993. Snow temperature patterns and artificial avalanche release. Proceedings of the 1992 International Snow Science Workshop in Breckenridge. (Colorado Avalanche Information Center, Denver, CO), 37-46.

11. C. Fraser. 1978. Avalanches and Snow Safety. John Murray Ltd., London, England, 269 pp.

12. B. Jamieson and C.D. Johnston. 1992. Snowpack characteristics associated with avalanche accidents. Canadian Geotechnical Journal 29, 862-866.

13. B. Jamieson and C. Johnston. 1997. The compression test for snow stability. Proceedings of the October 1996 International Snow Science Workshop in Banff, 118-125. (Canadian Avalanche Association, P.O. Box 2759, Revelstoke, BC, V0E 2S0, Canada.) Also abridged for Avalanche News 49, 12-15.

14. P.M.B. Föhn. 1987. The 'rutschblock' as a practical tool for slope stability evaluation in: Avalanche Formation, Movement and Effects, Eds. B. Salm and H. Gubler. IAHS Publication 162, 223-228.

15. B. Jamieson and C. Johnston. 1995. Interpreting rutschblocks in avalanche start zones. Avalanche News, 46, 2-4.

16. B. Jamieson and C. Johnston. 1992. Experience with rutschblocks. Avalanche Review 11(2). Also in Proceedings of the 1992 International Snow Science Workshop in Breckenridge. (Colorado Avalanche Information Center, Denver, CO), 150-159.

17. Canadian Avalanche Association. 1995. Observation Guidelines and Recording Standards for Weather, Snowpack and Avalanche Observations. (Canadian Avalanche Centre, P.O. Box 2759, Revelstoke, BC V0E 2S0), 107 pp.

18. A. Gleason. A comparison study of the Shredblock and Rutschblock snow stability tests. Proceedings of the 1998 International Snow Science Workshop in Sunriver, Oregon, 249-252 (Stevens Pass Ski Area, Skykomish, WA).

19. J. Fredston, D. Fesler and B. Tremper. 1995. The human factor - lessons for avalanche education. Proceedings of the International Snow Science Workshop at Snowbird, International Snow Science Workshop 1994, (P.O. Box 49, Snowbird, Utah 84092, USA), 473-486.

20. T. Auger and B. Jamieson. 1996. Avalanche probing revisited. Proceedings of the October 1996 International Snow Science Workshop in Banff, 295-298. (Canadian Avalanche Association, P.O. Box 2759, Revelstoke, V0E 2S0, BC, Canada.) Also reprinted in Avalanche News 49, 16-19.

21. B. Jamieson and T. Auger. Improved probing for buried avalanche victims. In press for Proceedings of the SAR Scene Conference in Sault Ste. Marie, October 1997.

22. S. Colbeck, E. Akitaya, R. Armstrong, H. Gubler, J. Lafeuille, K. Lied, D. McClung and E. Morris. 1990. International Classification for Seasonal Snow on the Ground. International Commission for Snow and Ice (IAHS), World Data Center A for Glaciology, U. of Colorado, Boulder, CO, USA.

23. P.A. Schaerer. 1987. Avalanche Accidents in Canada III. A Selection of Case Histories 1978-1984. (National Research Council of Canada, no. 27950), 183 pp.

Appendix A
Glossary

Aspect - The compass direction a slope faces. For example, a slope on the east side of a mountain has an east aspect.

Avalanche cycle - A period of avalanches associated with a storm or warm weather. For snow storms, the cycle typically starts during the storm and ends a few days after the storm.

Avalanche transceiver - An electronic device, roughly the size of your hand, worn by people in avalanche terrain. In transmit mode, it constantly transmits a radio signal which is stronger at closer range. If someone with a transmitting transceiver is buried, the other members of the group can switch their transceivers into receive mode and follow a search pattern that locates the strongest signal. The person is then found by probing and shoveling. (See also pages 50-53.)

Bed surface - The surface on which a slab avalanche runs. Not to be confused with failure layer. (See diagram on page 12.)

Cornice - An overhanging build-up of snow, usually on the lee side of ridges. Moderate or strong winds often create a vortex on the lee side and deposit wind-blown snow near the top of the lee slope. (See photos on pages 15 and 23.)

Cross-loaded - When wind blows across a cross-loaded slope, snow is picked up from the windward side of ribs and outcrops and is deposited in lee pockets. (See photo on page 32.)

Depth hoar - An advanced, generally larger, form of faceted crystal (see facets). Depth hoar crystals are striated and, in later stages, may be hollow. Cup-shaped crystals are a common form of depth hoar. This type of crystal can form at any level in the snowpack but is most commonly found at the base of shallow snowpacks following periods of cold weather. (See also page 63.)

Failure layer - Slab avalanches are released by a sequence of fractures. The first failure and fracture occurs in a weak layer called the failure layer. The fracture usually spreads along the top or bottom surface of the failure layer. The bed surface usually lies immediately below the failure layer. (See diagram on page 12.)

Facets (also called faceted crystals or sometimes *sugar snow*) - In response to a sufficiently strong temperature gradient within the snowpack, grains grow flat faces by a process know as *kinetic growth* or simply *faceting*. Facets commonly form near the snow surface or where the snowpack is shallow during periods of cold weather. (See also page 63.)

Melt-freeze crust - A layer of snow that has been warmed until liquid water forms between the grains and then freezes to form a relatively strong layer. Crusts sometimes form the *bed surface* for slab avalanches.

Propagation - The spreading of a fracture or crack. The shear fractures that spread along weak snow layers and release slab avalanches tend to propagate further under thicker, harder slabs than under thinner, softer slabs.

Rime - A deposit of ice from super-cooled water droplets. Rime can accumulate on the windward side of rocks, trees or structures, or on falling crystals of snow. When snow crystals cannot be recognised because of rime, the grains are called *graupel*.

Rounded grains (rounds) - Under sufficiently low *temperature gradients*, branched and angular crystals decompose into more rounded shapes called rounds. This dry-snow process involves the sublimation of ice from convex parts of grains into hollows. Rounding also tends to build bonds between grains (*sintering*). Consequently, layers of rounded grains are often stronger than layers of faceted grains of similar density. (See also page 63.)

Slab - One or more cohesive layers of snow that may start to slide together. (See photo and diagram on page 12.)

Sluff - A small avalanche usually made up of loose surface snow. (See photo on page 12.)

Snowpack - All the layers of snow on the ground.

Stepped down - A slab avalanche is said to step down if the motion of the initial slab causes lower layers to slide, resulting in a second bed surface deeper in the snowpack. A step in the bed surface is usually visible.

Storm snow - The snow that falls during a period of continuous or almost continuous snowfall. Many operations consider a storm to be over after a day with less than 1 cm of snow.

Sun crust - The term *sun crust* is often used to refer to a melt-freeze crust that is more noticeable on sunny slopes than on shady slopes. However, the international definition[22] is a thin, transparent layer (also called *firnspiegel*) caused by partial melting and refreezing of the surface layer.

Surface hoar - Crystals, often shaped like feathers, spikes or wedges, that grow upward from the snow surface when air just above the snow surface is cooled to the dew point. The winter equivalent of dew. Surface hoar grows most often when the wind is calm or light on cold, relatively clear nights. These crystals can also grow during the day on shady slopes. Once buried, layers of surface hoar are slow to gain strength, sometimes persisting for a month or more as potential failure planes for slab avalanches. (See photos on page 26.)

Temperature gradient - The temperature gradient is the change in temperature with depth in the snowpack. For example, if the temperature 20 cm below the surface is 3° warmer than the surface, then the temperature gradient in the top 20 cm averages 1.5° per 10 cm. Gradients greater than 1° per 10 cm are often associated with faceting of crystals and weakening of layers. Lower gradients are usually associated with rounding of grains and strengthening of layers. (See also page 64.)

Terrain trap - A terrain feature that increases the consequences of getting caught in an avalanche. For example, gullies and crevasses increase the odds of a deep burial, and cliffs increase the odds of traumatic injuries. (See also page 21)

Trigger - Anything that causes an avalanche to start. People, snowmobiles, cornice falls and explosives are *artificial* triggers. Natural avalanches are triggered by weather events such as warming or snowfall.

Whumpf - The sound of a fracture propagating along a weak layer within the snowpack. Whumpfs are indicators of local instability. In terrain steep enough to avalanche, whumpfs usually result in slab avalanches.

Wind-loaded - Terrain on which the wind has deposited additional snow. Slopes on the lee sides of ridges are often wind-loaded. (See also page 16)

Wind-slab - One or more stiff layers of wind-deposited snow. Wind slabs usually consist of snow crystals broken into small particles by the wind and packed together.

Photo by Selkirk Mountain Experience.

Appendix B
Snow Metamorphism

Dry Snow Metamorphism

There are two metamorphic processes in dry snow: rounding and faceting.

Rounding

In the rounding process (previously called equi-temperature or ET metamorphism) the grains become more blob-shaped and bond to neighboring grains. Part way through this process, when the original shapes of the new snow crystals can still be identified under a hand-held magnifier, the grains are called *partly decomposed* or *partly settled*. Because of the bonding between grains, **as the grains in a layer become rounder, the layers of these grains become progressively stronger.** During the rounding process, a snow layer will become denser and, over a period of days, settlement of the layer is often noticeable.

Faceting

In the faceting process, also called recrystallization or temperature gradient (TG) metamorphism, ice is deposited on the grains by the flow of water vapor through the snow. (Usually, the flow of water vapor is upwards and the ice is deposited on the bottom surfaces of the grains.) These deposits are first noticeable as corners on the grains and then as completely flat surfaces called *facets*. If the process continues, the grains will grow and take on a layered or stepped appearance. The final product of the process is an often-fragile layer consisting of large *depth hoar* grains. One of the most common forms of depth hoar is a hollow, cup-shaped grain. Depth hoar occurs most commonly at the bottom of thin snowpacks.

Rounding
(common in thick snowpack)

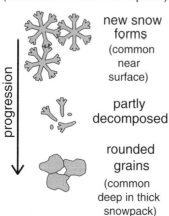

progression

new snow forms
(common near surface)

partly decomposed

rounded grains
(common deep in thick snowpack)

Faceting
(common in thin snowpack)

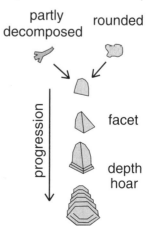

partly decomposed   rounded

progression

facet

depth hoar

In contrast to rounding, which bonds grains together and strengthens layers, **faceting usually forms few bonds between the grains and progressive weakening of snow layers may be noticeable over a period of days or weeks.**

Temperature gradient

The *temperature gradient* determines whether a layer will be strengthened by rounding or weakened by faceting. The temperature gradient is the vertical change in temperature within the snowpack. For example, if a 10 cm (4") thick layer is -3°C (27°F) on the bottom and -5°C (23°F) on top, then the temperature gradient within that layer is 2°C per 10 cm (4°F per 4").

Consider a snow layer, which like most layers in mid-winter, is somewhat cooler on top than on the bottom. If the temperature difference between the top and bottom of the layer is large, the gradient will draw water vapor up through the snow layer, causing faceting of the grains and probably weakening of the layer. However, if there is little temperature difference between the top and bottom of the layer, the temperature gradient will not draw water vapor through the snow fast enough to cause faceting; the grains will become rounder and the layer will strengthen.

Melt-Freeze Metamorphism

When snow is warmed to 0°C (32°F) by rain, solar radiation or warm air, rounded grains will develop which are joined into clusters by liquid water. This grain structure is weak, but it will form into a comparatively strong crust when the layer is frozen. In the spring, when melt-freeze cycles are repeated daily, the resulting *spring snow* has a coarse-grained appearance.

Melt-Freeze
(common during thaws, spring)

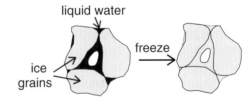

Appendix C
Avalanche Danger Scales

Canadian Avalanche Danger Scale

AVALANCHE SAFETY BASICS

Avalanches don't happen by accident and most human involvement is a matter of **choice**, not chance. Most avalanche accidents are caused by **slab** avalanches which are triggered by the victim or by a member of the victim's party. However, **any** avalanche may cause injury or death and even small slides may be dangerous. Hence, always practise safe route-finding skills, be aware of changing conditions, and carry avalanche rescue gear. Learn and apply avalanche terrain analysis and snow stability evaluation techniques to help minimize your risk. Remember that avalanche danger rating levels are only general guidelines. Distinctions between geographic areas, elevations, slope aspects and slope angles are approximate and transition zones between dangers exist.

Canadian Avalanche Danger Descriptors

Danger Level (& Color)	Avalanche Probability and Avalanche Trigger	Recommended Action in the Backcountry
…WHAT…	…WHY…	…WHAT TO DO…
LOW (green)	Natural avalanches very unlikely. Human-triggered avalanches **unlikely**.	Travel is generally safe. Normal caution advised.
MODERATE (yellow)	Natural avalanches unlikely. Human-triggered avalanches **possible**.	Use caution in steeper terrain on certain aspects (defined in accompanying statement).
CONSIDERABLE (orange)	Natural avalanches possible. Human-triggered avalanches **probable**.	Be increasingly cautious in steeper terrain.
HIGH (red)	Natural and human-triggered avalanches **likely**.	Travel in avalanche terrain is not recommended.
EXTREME (red with black border)	Widespread natural or human-triggered avalanches **certain**.	Travel in avalanche terrain should be avoided and travel confined to low angle terrain well away from avalanche runouts.

United States Avalanche Danger Scale

AVALANCHE SAFETY BASICS

Avalanches don't happen by accident and most human involvement is a matter of **choice**, not chance. Most avalanche accidents are caused by **slab** avalanches which are triggered by the victim or by a member of the victim's party. However, **any** avalanche may cause injury or death and even small slides may be dangerous. Hence, always practise safe route finding skills, be aware of changing conditions, and carry avalanche rescue gear. Learn and apply avalanche terrain analysis and snow stability evaluation techniques to help minimize your risk. Remember that avalanche danger rating levels are only general guidelines. Distinctions between geographic areas, elevations, slope aspects and slope angles are approximate and transition zones between dangers exist. No matter what the current avalanche danger there are avalanche-safe areas in the mountains.

United States Avalanche Danger Descriptors

Danger Level (& Color)	Avalanche Probability and Avalanche Trigger	Degree and Distribution of Avalanche Danger	Recommended Action in the Backcountry
…WHAT…	…WHY…	…WHERE…	…WHAT TO DO…
LOW (green)	Natural avalanches very unlikely. Human-triggered avalanches **unlikely**.	Generally stable snow. Isolated areas of instability.	Travel is generally safe. Normal caution advised.
MODERATE (yellow)	Natural avalanches unlikely. Human-triggered avalanches **possible**.	Unstable slabs **possible** on steep terrain.	Use caution in steeper terrain on certain aspects (defined in accompanying statement).
CONSIDERABLE (orange)	Natural avalanches possible. Human-triggered avalanches **probable**.	Unstable slabs **probable** on steep terrain.	Be increasingly cautious in steeper terrain.
HIGH (red)	Natural and human-triggered avalanches **likely**.	Unstable slabs **likely** on a variety of aspects and slope angles.	Travel in avalanche terrain is not recommended. Safest travel on windward ridges of lower angle slopes without steeper terrain above.
EXTREME (red with black border)	Widespread natural or human-triggered avalanches **certain**.	Extremely unstable slabs **certain** on most aspects and slope angles. Large destructive avalanches possible.	Travel in avalanche terrain should be avoided and travel confined to low-angle terrain well away from avalanche runouts.

Appendix D
Classifying the Size of Avalanches

Canadian Classification for Avalanche Size[6]

Size Destructive Potential

1   Relatively harmless to people.

2   Could bury, injure or kill a person.

3   Could bury and destroy a car, damage a truck, destroy a small building or break a few trees.

4   Could destroy a railway car, large truck, several buildings or a forest area up to 4 hectares (~10 acres).

5   Largest snow avalanche known. Could destroy a village or a forest of 40 hectares (~100 acres).

Half-sizes from 1.5 to 4.5 may be used for avalanches that are between two size classes.

United States Classification for Avalanche Size[6]

Size Description

1   Sluff or snow that slides less than 50 m (150') of slope distance, regardless of snow volume.

2   Small, relative to path.

3   Medium, relative to path.

4   Large, relative to path.

5   Major or maximum, relative to path.

Appendix E
Sources for Current Avalanche Conditions

Phone Numbers (USA)

(530) 587-2158	Lake Tahoe/Donner Summit Area (Truckee, California)
(760) 924-5500	Central-eastern Sierra (Mammoth Lakes, California)
(406) 257-8402	Northwest Montana Rockies (Whitefish, Montana)
(406) 587-6981	South Central Mountains (Bozeman, Montana)
(406) 838-2341	Southern Mountains (Cooke City, Montana)
(406) 646-7912	Southern Mountains (West Yellowstone, Montana)
(307) 733-2664	Teton and Wind River Mountains, Wyoming
(208) 788-1200 x 8027	Sun Valley, ID
(206) 526-6677	Washington Cascades and Olympics (Seattle, WA)
(503) 808-2400	S. Washington Cascades and Mt. Hood (Portland, OR)
(801) 378-4333	Sundance / Mt. Timpanogos Area (Provo, Utah)
(801) 364-1581	Tri-Canyon Area, (Salt Lake City, Utah)
(435) 658-5512	Park City Area, Utah
(801) 742-0830	Alta, Utah
(801) 626-8700	Mt. Ogden and South, Utah
(801) 797-4146	North Wasatch Mountains (Logan, Utah)
(801) 259-7669	La Sal Mountains (Moab, Utah)
(303) 275-5360	Colorado Rockies (Denver / Boulder)
(970) 482-0457	Colorado Rockies (Fort Collins)
(970) 668-0600	Colorado Rockies (Summit County)
(719) 520-0020	Colorado Rockies (Colorado Springs)
(970) 827-5687	Colorado Rockies (Vail)
(970) 827-5687	Holy Cross Ranger District, Colorado
(970) 920-1664	Colorado Rockies (Aspen)
(970) 247-8187	Colorado Rockies (Durango)
(603) 466-2713	Tuckerman and Huntington Ravines, New Hampshire

Phone Numbers (Canada)

(800) 667-1105	Canadian Avalanche Centre for Rockies, Columbia Mtns & South Coast of BC
(403) 762-1460	Banff, Kootenay & Yoho National Parks
(250) 814-5232	Glacier National Park (Rogers Pass)
(780) 852-6176	Jasper National Park

Web Sites

Web sites with information for many areas

Canadian Avalanche Centre   www.avalanche.ca/

Westwide Avalanche Network   www.avalanche.org/

Cyberspace Snow and Avalanche Center   www.csac.org/

Web sites with local information (Canada)

Glacier National Park
www.avalanche.ca/glacier.htm

Banff, Yoho and Kootenay National Parks
discoveralberta.com/ParksCanada-Banff/AvalancheInfo/

Jasper National Park
discoveralberta.com/ParksCanada-Jasper/AvalancheInfo/

Waterton Lakes National Park
discoveralberta.com/ParksCanada-Waterton/AvalancheInfo/

Kananaskis Country
www.gov.ab.ca/env/parks/prov_parks/kananaskis/safety/backreport.html

Web sites with local information (USA)

Tuckerman and Huntington Ravines	www.mountwashington.org/avalanche/
SW Montana (Bozeman)	www.gomontana.com/avalanche/
Missoula, Montana	www.fs.fed.us/r1/lolo/rec-contrib/advisory.htm
NW Montana (Glacier)	www.avalanche.org/~gnfac/gcac-bulletin.txt
Sun Valley, Idaho	www.avalanche.org/~ciac/bulletin.txt
Southeastern Idaho	www.usu.edu/~uafclogn/adv2.HTM
Idaho Panhandle	www.fs.fed.us/outernet/ipnf/avalanche.html
Washington & Oregon	www.nwn.noaa.gov/sites/nwac
Jackson, Wyoming	www.sisna.com/jackson/bcaf/
Truckee (Central Sierra), Calif.	www.r5.pswfs.gov/tahoe/avalanche.html
Colorado	www.caic.state.co.us/report.asp
Logan (N. Wasatch), Utah	www.usu.edu/~uafclogn/adv1.HTM
Moab, Utah	www.avalanche.org/~lsafc/
Salt Lake City, Utah	www.avalanche.org/~uafc/index.phtml

for icons & visual presentation

Appendix F
Reporting Avalanche Incidents

Courtesy of Canadian Avalanche Association

Objective

The objective of reporting avalanche incidents and damage is to collect data about the extent of avalanche problems in Canada. Summaries of the reports will draw attention to avalanche dangers and assist in the development of safety measures.

Reporting Forms

Two different reporting forms are available for recording avalanche incidents and damage.

The *concise form* is designed for reporting the fact that people or objects had an encounter with avalanches. This short report should be submitted every time people are involved in an avalanche or property is damaged. A blank avalanche involvement reporting form is included in this appendix.

The *detailed reporting form* allows the characteristics of the avalanche and details about the event to be recorded. The detailed report should be completed primarily for the records of the operation concerned, either when an avalanche caused a fatality, serious injury, or property damage in excess of $10 000 or when the incident has a high educational value. It may be useful as a checklist when operations may wish to describe an accident and the rescue work in greater detail. Blank forms are available from the Canadian Avalanche Centre.

Filing of Reports

Completed concise reports should be returned as quickly as possible to the Canadian Avalanche Centre in Revelstoke, British Columbia.

The individual reports will be treated confidentially and the results will be made public in summary form only. Interesting cases will be included in publications of avalanche accident case histories, if the concerned reporters and involved persons and companies agree. The names of the reporters or victims are not required.

Completion of the Short Form

1. Date and Time

Fill in the date and time of the avalanche occurrence.

2. Location

Give the name of the mountain area, highway, or ski area and either a description, name, or number of the avalanche path.

3. Avalanche Description

Fill out the appropriate fields to the best of your knowledge.

4. Number of People

Enter the total number of people in the party and how many of them were either caught, partially buried or completely buried in the avalanche. Indicate how many people were injured or killed.

Under this section enter the number of people in buildings or vehicles buried or damaged by the avalanche.

Note: The number of injured and dead people must be included in the numbers caught, partially buried and buried:

A person is <u>caught only</u> if he is touched by the avalanche but not covered with snow when the avalanche stops.

A person is <u>partially buried</u> if any part of the body is visible on the surface when the avalanche stops. People in vehicles which are partially buried must be reported here.

A person is <u>completely buried</u> if he is completely beneath the snow surface when the avalanche stops. Equipment such as skis or poles may be visible on the surface. People in vehicles which are buried must be reported here.

5. Activity of People

Write the type of activity being done by the people at the time of the avalanche for those that were caught or partially or completely buried; e.g. skiing, snowmobiling, mountain climbing, avalanche control, travel on the road, snow plowing.

6. Number of Vehicles

Indicate the number of vehicles that were either trapped, partially buried or buried. Indicate how many of them were damaged.

Note: Vehicles include those on roads, rails, as well as over-snow vehicles and aircraft.

A vehicle is <u>trapped</u> if it is blocked by avalanche deposits in front of and behind it, or if it became stuck when it tried to cross or ran into an avalanche deposit.

A vehicle is <u>partially buried</u> if any part is still visible when the avalanche stops.

A vehicle is <u>buried</u> if it is completely beneath the snow surface when the avalanche stops.

7. Structures Damaged

Enter the number and type of structural damages. For example, include the function and construction type of buildings, the number of poles and length of telephone line or power line, the type of lift towers, a bridge, etc. Estimate the loss in dollar terms whenever possible.

8. Estimated Depth of Burial

For buried people and vehicles, give the depth between the highest part of the body or vehicle and the avalanche surface.

9. Estimated Duration of Burial

Estimate the time between the occurrence of the avalanche and when the person or object was uncovered.

10. Comments

Make brief notes on the principal cause of the avalanche encounter. Examples include the weather (snowfall, wind, temperature), snow conditions, skiers entering a closed area and triggering the avalanche.

CANADIAN AVALANCHE ASSOCIATION

Avalanche Involvement Report

(Concise form)

DATE (year, month, day) _____

TIME (hour, min) _____ : ___ (24 hr clock)

LOCATION _____

AVALANCHE DESCRIPTION
Size (1.0 to 5.0) __.__   Elevation _____
Aspect _____   Incline _____
Type (check one) Loose __Slab __   Slab Width ____   Thickness ___.__
Liquid Water in Deposit (check one) Dry __   Moist __   Wet __
Trigger _____
Sliding Layer (If known) _____

PEOPLE	Number of People	Number of People Wearing Transceivers		
		457 kHz	2.275 kHz	Dual
Total in party	_____	_____	_____	_____
Caught only	_____	_____	_____	_____
Partially buried	_____	_____	_____	_____
Completely buried	_____	_____	_____	_____
Injured	_____	_____	_____	_____
Fatalities	_____	_____	_____	_____

ACTIVITY OF PEOPLE _____

EQUIPMENT LOST _____
VEHICLES (number)
Trapped _____   Partially Buried _____
Completely Buried _____   Damaged _____
Type of Vehicles

STRUCTURES DAMAGED _____

Estimated total property loss $ _____ , _____ , _____.00

Estimated Depth of Burial (m)   _____.__   _____.__   _____.__
Estimated Duration of Burial (hrs, min) _____ : ___   _____ : ___   _____ : ___
COMMENTS (Snowpack, Burial, Search and Rescue details, please attach additional pages if necessary.): _____

Name and address of reporter (Can the CAA contact you for further information?)
_____
_____

Please send as soon as possible to: Canadian Avalanche Centre
                                        PO Box 2759, Revelstoke, British Columbia V0E 2S0
                                        Fax: (250) 837-4624   Phone: (250) 837-2435
Note: This information will be used for public education and information. It may be summarized and published by the CAC. The reporter's name will not be published by the CAA.

Appendix G
Incident Response

This form can be carried in your first aid kit and used at a backcountry incident.

Remember to calmly assess the situation, appoint a leader and—if safety permits—locate victims and provide first aid. If additional help is required, decide who should stay at the accident site and who should seek assistance, and send this completed form out with the messengers.

Date: Time: Terrain:

Accident location (mark on map):	
Possible location for helicopter to land (mark on map):	
Description of accident:	
Number of injured persons:	
First injured person	Second injured person
Name: Condition: Length of time unconscious:	
Injury 1: Treatment:	
Injury 2: Treatment:	
Number of uninjured persons: General condition: Requirements: water food shelter warm clothing	

Appendix H
Equipment Checklist
for Day Trip

Group Survival Gear

repair kit
first aid kit
pocket knife
waterproof matches or lighter
fire starter
high-energy food
headlamp, spare bulb and battery
foam pad
bivvy sack/emergency shelter
rope and parts for improvised
    toboggan (for remote areas)
map, compass and pencil
altimeter (optional)
GPS receiver (optional)
two-way radios (optional)
personal locator beacon (remote areas)

Repair Kit

mini-tool or screwdriver and pliers
spare screws for bindings
electrical/duct tape
wire
cord
needle and thread

Snow Kit (optional)

snow saw
knotted cord for cutting rutschblocks
clinometer
magnifier
crystal screen
ruler
field book and pencil
thermometer

First Aid Kit

triangular bandages
pressure bandage
sterile pads
adhesive bandages (small & large)
alcohol wipes
butterfly bandages
aspirin or acetominophen tablets
adhesive tape
scissors
tweezers

Personal Gear

transceiver, probe & shovel
snowboard and snowshoes
(or split board and skins)
telescoping poles
boots
long underwear and socks
shirt or sweater
windproof jacket & pants
extra sweater
helmet or warm hat
gloves or mitts
backpack and straps for board
lunch and snacks
thermos and water/juice/tea
sunscreen, lip protector
goggles and/or shades
toilet paper
pocket knife
camera and film
money and personal ID
medications